Library of Congress Cat. Card No. 73-89352
ISBN 0-913642-05-3
10 9 8 7 6 5 4 3 2 1

Printed in the United States of America

BALAMP PUBLISHING
7430 Second Blvd.
Detroit, Michigan 48202

'YOU DON'T LOOK LIKE A MUSICIAN'

BUD FREEMAN
Jazz saxophonist

BALAMP PUBLISHING
Detroit, Michigan

CONTENTS

JAZZ ABROAD

iv

SOCIOLOGY AND ALL THAT JAZZ!

THINGS TO THINK ON

HERE AND THERE

FOREWORD

This book is about all the wonderful, crazy people I've known in the forty-nine years I've been playing. My life has been very interesting and rich. In fact, I wish that I could afford to live the way I live, but if I could afford to live the way I live, I'd hate to spend my own money!

Frank Angelo, Executive Editor of the *Detroit Free Press*, wrote an article about me. During an interview, Frank suggested that I tell my readers about jazz: what is it? I said that there is no way to describe jazz; that I'd rather tell how it differs from other kinds of music, and what powerful therapy it has. Although it is a kind of music come of oppression, it has the charm to make its listeners happy.

My sincere thanks to Nancy Kennedy, without whose encouragement I could never have written this book. I want also to thank Kay Savage, the famous Food Editor, for introducing me to Nancy.

BUD FREEMAN

August, 1973

MOSTLY ABOUT ME

MUSICAL ENVIRONMENT

My mother had five sisters and two brothers. They all played the piano. Since my mother was the only one on her side of the family to have a house with piano, they all sort of congregated there. I cannot remember a day when there wasn't someone playing the piano. My father had been in the Spanish American War. I'm not certain whether or not he played the drums, but he owned a pair of authentic army drumsticks which I used to drum on a chair. They said that I had a good beat. I suppose it's true because later when I began to play the saxophone, that beat came in very handily since I could only play one note. Incidentally, I have never had the desire to be a drummer. Just the thought of carrying all of those contraptions around wearied me.

I first became aware of my love for music at the age of eight. The next four years were spent completely resenting the idea of having to go to school My only interests were music, the movies and sports. When I reached the age of thirteen, it appeared that they were having a difficult time talking me into graduating. I entered an all-city track meet and won all of the events. My father received a letter from the school principal who suggested that my athletic talent was not ordinary. On the strength of this I was graduated and enrolled at Austin High School. In my first track event, I was so far behind all of the other runners that I had the feeling I was running in the wrong direction. I didn't care especially. My father was a good athlete, and I suppose I wanted to please him.

Every Friday after classes there was a dance held in the social room. Now Austin High School was unique in that there were quite a few professional musicians attending it. These musicians played a few days a week at ballrooms and private parties and offered their services for nothing at school just because they loved to play. I never missed a Friday. Without any musical experience up to that point, I felt that I knew everything they were doing. A little man from Oak Park High School used to come over to Austin to meet his girl. I was fascinated with the way they danced and dressed. The collegiate look was the thing and they had it. One Friday the musicians asked the little man to sit in and everybody gathered around applauding like mad. The little man was none other than Dave Tough, the great drummer who was later to lead all the bop drummers in what *they* thought was a new style. Dave had already been playing professionally a couple of years. I pushed my way through the crowd and shoved my hand out to him. He treated me as though I were a pro. Also attending Austin were the McPartland brothers (Jimmy and Dick), and Jim Lanigan who later married their sister. I had no idea at that time that I would play an instrument. I just knew that I loved it and actually idolized anyone who could play. Eventually, I did meet the McPartland brothers who were very influential in talking my father into buying me a saxophone.

My first saxophone was a brass C-melody. It was to me, a most precious gem. I was afraid to blow it for fear of marring it. I took some lessons from Jimmy McPartland's father. I didn't like the lessons. They reminded me of grammar school. I suppose I expected the horn to play by itself. I had a lot of music in my head. I was *so* disappointed that it didn't come out of the horn. There were periods when I didn't touch it for weeks, but I never missed the opportunity to hear what was happening in music. Dick McPartland taught me chords and I tried to play things that I couldn't finger. Whenever I was hung up, I'd get on one note and play different rhythm patterns on it. A long period of time passed before I could play a melody.

MY FIRST JOB

The first time I tried to play professionally, I was nearly murdered for it. Dave Tough (the famous drummer who was later to become a deep influence on me) had just received an offer to play at a road house in Sheybogan, Wisconsin for the summer season. Dave liked me as a friend and told the man, an ex-vaudeville pianist who had the job that I was the finest C-melody sax man around. The man, of course, asked Dave Tough if I would audition for the job and Dave knowing that the audition would be disastrous simply said that I was too much an artist to audition whereupon the man hired me on the strength of Dave's word. The road house was one of the last of the old style saloons. It had that smell of whiskey and beer stained in wood. There was a bar and nightclub which were separated by two swinging doors. The customers were usually college students, lumber jacks, and an Indian who used to wrestle the bartender every night for drinks. We played from 9 at night until 1:00 a. m. and, of course, the pianist would go out of his mind with me and he'd tell Dave every night that I had to go and Dave would say if Bud leaves I leave. Finally it got so bad that Dave couldn't take it anymore and left to take another job. On the night Dave left, the pianist grabbed me by the throat and screamed, "You son of a bitch; if you're not out of town in an hour, I'll murder you." While the job lasted, I did rather well financially. It paid $40 a week which was equivalent to $400 a week today. My rent in a boarding house was $3.50 a week, and come to think of it, I'm not doing any better today!

VAUDEVILLE

In 1925 I was playing with what was left of the Old Wolverines. This was the band that the great Bix had made famous. The original members had all left and George Wettling the great drummer and I played a few vaudeville houses with the band for practically no money at all. We had to start somewhere and we were happy just to be playing. We had a girl dancer featured in our act, and one night we had to follow a trained seal act. The seal act was the usual act where the seal balanced balls on his nose and played a tune on an instrument. (Incidentally, I think that seals are the worst musicians I've ever heard. I've never heard one play a tune without making a mistake.) Now in this act there was a wooden tank of water for the seal to swim in, and of course water was splashed all over the stage. At the end of this act, no one thought to mop the stage. Just off of the stage was

4

the men's toilet, and as our dancer made her entrance, she slipped and ended up there. This actually broke up the audience and the manager insisted that we leave it in the act. The girl quit and that was the end of my Vaudeville career.

CONSOLATION

Back in the twenties when I was learning how to play, I worked in many places that were owned by bootleggers and gunmen. One of the owners, a certain Tony D. noticed that I was a little frightened of the environment and in an effort to comfort me, put his arm around me and said, "Buddy, don't ever worry about anybody in this here joint because *nobody* in this here joint will hurt you unless he gets paid for it."

LETTER FROM MY BROTHER, THE ACTOR

"Listen, I've got a great idea for us. When we're 82 and 85 respectively, we'll rent Santa Claus outfits, stand in front of Macy's and you play the horn and I'll do recitations. We'll clean up. What other Santas can compete with us? — Those old drunks. And we'll only have to work a couple of weeks a year. So don't worry."

THE IMPECUNIOUS DAYS

In the early thirties Dave Tough, the great drummer, and I were freelancing in New York, which simply means that we were out of work. One day we got a call from the Dorsey brothers to play what is called a sound-track date. In this case it was to synchronize the music for a moving picture. The day's pay came to ninety dollars a-piece, the most money we had seen in weeks. Instead of trying to save some of the money until more work came in, we went out on the town and blew it all in one night. The next day we didn't have enough money left to buy a tube of toothpaste, and when I mentioned this to Dave, he said, "We can afford the luxuries of life, but never the necessities."

MY BROTHER ARNY

When my brother Arny (who was later to become an

5

actor) and I were in our teens, we were not very ambitious in the way that most people think they're supposed to be, but rather we were ambitious about a way of life. We lived in a community where neighbors were forever butting into one another's business to the extent of even asking my father why his boys didn't go to work. My father would reply, "You don't understand; my boys are different." After having been brain-washed by the community, my father came into our room at seven one morning and announced, "You boys are getting up and going out to look for jobs and amount to something like other people." My brother's answer to this outrageous suggestion was :"How dare you wake us up before the weekend!" My father left without saying a word.

SUMMA CUM LAUDE

At the end of 1939 I left Benny Goodman's band, vowing that I'd never again work for another band leader. I have never broken my vow. I had no idea what I was going to do. The idea of having my own band, especially in view of what I'd been through with Tommy Dorsey and Benny Goodman, horrified me. In the few times that I tried to have a band I was so embarrassed that I used to stand *behind* it. Now Eddie Condon had a band playing at "Nick's" in Greenwich Village. In the band were Eddie on guitar, Pee Wee Russell on clarinet, Brad Gowans on valve trombone, Dave Bowman on piano, Maxie Kaminsky on trumpet and, now and then, the great Dave Tough on drums. Ernie Anderson, who was later to become John Huston's public relations director, called me one day and suggested that since I had had so much publicity, would I consider fronting Eddie Condon's band. I would have no responsibilities, other than to play, he promised. I jumped at the offer and opened as the leader a week later. Phyllis Condon, Eddie's wife, a brilliant woman, named the band "Bud Freeman and the *Summa Cum Laude*." The business jumped from good to sensational in a month. Incidentally, our band acted as a rehearsal band for several bass players — I think we had six of them in the seven months we played at Nick's. Two, whose names I recall were Clyde Newcombe and Clyde Lombardi. Never had a night gone by that some world famous

6

person did not come in to hear the band. Nick's became the hangout for such celebrities as John Steinbeck, Spencer Tracy, The Dorsey brothers, Joe DiMaggio, Willem De Kooning the painter, Lipshitz the sculptor, Tallulah Bankhead, Peter Arno, Paul Whiteman, Igor Stravinsky, and "Willie Sutton" with his latest face.

After about seven months of having done fabulous business, we were offered a job in a show called "Swinging the Dream." Eric Charell, who had had great success in Europe with a show called, "Whitehorse Inn," had an idea to combine "Shakespeare" with "Swing." We were to play a sort of Jazz band entracte and Benny Goodman was to feature his quintette. The other names in the show were Louis Armstrong, Maxine Sullivan, Dorothy Maguire (the well known actress), Bill Bailey (the great tap dancer), "Butterfly MacQueen" (the actress), "Troy Brown" the 400 pound comedian and dancer, "Nicodemus" of "Amos and Andy" fame, and Don Voorhees the well known conductor who had the band in the pit. Never in the history of show business had there been so much talent put together in one show and never had so much talent had so short a run. It ran exactly eleven days. I don't think that the producer had the faintest idea of what he was doing. If he had just put all of these artists together in a revue, the show might still be running. One day at rehearsal, just before the show closed, it dawned on him that he was losing a fortune and had better start cutting people out. I was the first victim and this was the excuse he presented to me: "Mr. Freeman, your band she is too loud. I want you to play soft like Count Basie."

THE BLACK MAN'S MUSIC

The first time I ever heard a black man play, I was about seventeen and my friend Dave Tough who had been exposed to this music for some time took me out to a place in the black section of Chicago called the Lincoln Gardens. The band was led by the great King Oliver, the first great Jazz trumpet player. There was an unknown second cornet player in the band by the name of Louis Armstrong. Lil Armstrong, the pianist, was Louis' wife. Dutrey was the trombone player, Johnny Dodds was the clarinet player and his brother "Baby" was the drummer.

I had never heard any music so creative and exciting as this band played; I had not yet begun to play an instrument and I really believe that hearing all this was the greatest education in music I've ever had. I was not only hearing a new form of music but was experiencing a whole new way of life. Here were these beautiful people, not allowed any of the privileges of the white man, and yet they seemed to be so much freer in spirit and so much more relaxed than the white man. I think I was impressed with the black man's way of life at an early age because he seemed so much wiser than the white man. That is to say, he refused to be brainwashed by all the ideas that the white man was brainwashed into believing. Certainly there can be no doubt that guilt and ego have done more to destroy man than anything else. In the many years that I've been associated with the black man I've found that he takes each day as it comes and doesn't worry about tomorrow. I feel very fortunate to have heard his music at an early age. My life has been enriched by it.

THE WORLD'S GREATEST JAZZ BAND

To my knowledge there has *never* been a business arrangement in the history of the music business where every member of a band shared equally in its profits. Several years ago a gentleman by the name of Richard Gibson, a devout lover of Jazz music, gave a party in Aspen, Colorado where several Jazz musicians, all of whom were famous, were hired to perform. The party ran for three days and was strictly invitational. The guests were obviously more wealthy than poor since the expense for each invited guest was quite high. The invitation simply meant that the guests were on a Gibson mailing list, but since they were rabid Jazz fans, they looked upon this invitation as a privilege, no matter what the expense to themselves. Now, the musicians also looked upon this as a privilege, because there were very few opportunities to play the kind of music they loved and at the same time be very well paid. The parties were a tremendous success musically, but I'm certain that Dick Gibson must have lost money on each one of them. In his own words, "I'm not doing this to make money." After several years of giving these parties and seeing the tremendous response, Dick decided to raise money to finance an all-star band, each musician to receive the same salary and a percentage of the profits. Obviously, the payroll for such a band would run into several thousand dollars a week. Now at this time it appeared that the bottom had dropped out of the music business and surely no operators of night-clubs or hotels would spend this kind of money. So Dick came up with the money. This meant that the musicians had to be paid a very high salary, so that when the band was not working it seemed most logical, from a monetary point of view, to stay on. We opened up in New York and from the very inception the band was a howling success. Of course, there was a small fortune spent on publicity alone.

Now, the unique thing about Jazz music is that it picks up a lot of free publicity around the world and people feel a great need to identify with it. As a result of this our band became, in as short a time as a month, the most talked of band in existence. In less than a year we played every major television show in the country and jammed people into every place we played. Dick Gibson named the band "The World's Greatest Jazz Band" simply because he thought so. The band is made up of nine world famous soloists, each of whom has his own following. It is most unique because each player has his own individual style giving us a varied repertoire. In my opinion there has never been anything like it. It may or may not be known by the lover of Jazz music that musicians have rarely been happy in their work because of the rat race of the music business. *Isn't it strange that patrons of the arts for years on end have never given a thought to subsidizing the only true American art form, Jazz music.* It would appear that if they thought about it at all, which I doubt, they must have thought that any bum could play Jazz. Jazz music is the only kind of music that has the power to take one out of a state of despondency. I know, because I've tested this in listening to every kind of music ever played. If one is happy, Jazz makes one happier. If one is despondent, Jazz gives one a lift.

At this writing, I regret to say that Dick Gibson has just sold all of his stock in the band to stay at home in Denver to look after his family of a lovely wife and four adorable children. Without Dick's love for Jazz, this band could never have been organized.

OH . . . TO BE SIXTY AGAIN

For years on end, people have been asking me my age. For the edification of those who are still alive, I should like to say that I'm not certain how old I am, but just recently a lady about fifty years of age came backstage to say "hello." She looked up at me and said, "Mr. Freeman, my mother said to say 'hello' to you."

THE DAY WE "HELD UP" THE BANK IN KENOSHA

Our band was playing a string of concerts throughout the country and whenever we're on tour our paychecks are sent ahead to a given hotel so that we're always paid on time. There's an odd thing about musicians: they always need money. Bob Haggart, who distributes the checks, usually checks out the bank that is most available and the men cash their checks at their own leisure. I do not recall that we had ever gone all together at one time, until the day we played in Kenosha. We didn't get into town until just before the bank was to close and so we rushed over en masse. Now the clothes that we wear for traveling in a bus do not exactly present a picture of sartorial splendor, what with boots, stocking caps, dark sun glasses, leather jackets, turtleneck sweaters and what not, so that the nine of us must have appeared to the bank employees as a gang of bank robbers. It looked like the real thing to them, especially since bank robbery is so fashionable today. Our checks are always certified and I'm certain that any bank executive can tell a good check from a bad one, but since the amount came to several thousand dollars it could easily look like an original idea in bank robbery. But Bob Haggart presented our contract for the concert we were to play that night and asked the head man at the bank to call the man who had hired us to play. As it turned out everything was OK'd, but for several long minutes we were completely covered by every eye in the bank. Every employee in the bank seemed to stop doing what he was doing until we left. It's a pity that bank robbers don't get any fun out of their work. I enjoyed it.

10

YOU DON'T LOOK LIKE A MUSICIAN

For years on end people have been telling me that I don't look like a musician; that I look like a banker. Now what do they mean to imply? Do they mean to imply that musicians look like bums? A musician can only look like a musician when he's playing music. Do they mean that he looks unkempt? That he is ill mannered? The most clothes-conscious, immaculate people I've ever known are musicians. As regards bankers, I've never seen a distinguished looking banker, unless he was the president of the bank and, of course, had that rich look that people with money have. Bankers, as a matter of fact, are quite ordinary looking people.

Musicians are not as highly regarded as other artists because their art is not as obvious. You can't see music, and as strange as it may seem, people don't listen as much as they look. The musician with some form of showmanship has always become the most popular. I wonder if people will ever learn to listen to music. Incidentally, the day we "held up" the bank in Kenosha, we didn't look very much like musicians.

11

JAZZ GREATS

THE GREAT LOUIS AND THE MASTERS

What can be said about the master that hasn't been said? In my opinion he was the father of Jazz music. Almost every phrase in Jazz played today can be traced back to Louis' playing. I would strongly advise any young musician who has an interest in Jazz to start with the early recordings of Louis Armstrong and the HOT FIVE. I realize that there are courses in Jazz now being taught in many schools throughout the country, but to me the best way to develop an interest would surely be in listening to the Jazz masters on records. My suggestions would be — Bessie Smith, Ethel Waters, Louis Armstrong, Sidney Bechet, James P. Johnson, Fats Waller, Bix, King Oliver, Dave Tough, Sid Catlett, Fletcher Henderson, and Duke Ellington as a start. To my knowledge these were the most creative of their time. There are, of course, many others that I could mention such as Jelly Roll Morton and Willie the Lion Smith, but listening to these greats will lead to others as one's interest develops.

THE POWER OF LOUIS ARMSTRONG

In the last 45 years there has *not* been a soloist in Jazz music who was not influenced by Louis Armstrong. I speak *only* of the soloists who became great themselves. To begin, "Bunny Berigan": Listen particularly to his solo on the recording of "Marie" with Tommy Dorsey, "Hot Lips" Page, Buck Clayton, Charlie Shavers, Harry James before he became a ballad player, and Rex Stewart when he was very young. Bobby Hackett's style is very melodic and soft, but I hear a very strong Armstrong influence in it. Billy Butterfield (the best ballad player in the world) plays like Louie at times. Dizzy Gillespie, Miles Davis, and Roy Eldridge have talked to me at great length about Armstrong's influence on them. Coleman Hawkins completely changed his style after hearing Louie. Lester Young had a beat that was Louie's. Fats Waller, Earl Hines, Jess Stacy, Ralph Sutton, Joe Bushkin, Art Tatum, Teddy Wilson, Count Basie, and Duke Ellington spent hours on end listening to Louie. I played a concert tour of Great Britain a few years ago with Ben Webster and Eddie Miller; the talk was always about Louie. I could go on and on endlessly writing about Louis Armstrong's influence on other great players. He was indeed the most powerful voice in American music.

LOUIE AND THE SUNSET CAFE

In the middle twenties Joe Glaser (who later became Louis Armstrong's manager) owned a nite-club on the south side of Chicago. It was called the "Sunset Cafe." It featured the Carrol Dickerson Orchestra and a floor show. The show had the usual master-of-ceremonies who told a few jokes and ended his routine with a tap-dance. There was a chorus of girls who could *really* dance and sing and there were very funny comedians, most of whom were to become famous in the Amos and Andy television series. A few of these who made the big time were Nicodemus, Troy Brown, Buck and Bubbles, Valaida Snow, Pigmeat Markham, and a dance team called Brown & McGraw, the finest black husband and wife team I've ever seen. There were also Nicholas Brothers (the finest acrobatic dancers I've ever seen), and Rector & Cooper, an excellent dance team. A little man (by the name of Percy Venable) produced and directed the floor show. If he had lived longer (he died at an early age) he would have become one of the greats; his shows were way ahead of their time. His partner was Lucius Millinder, later to become famous as Lucky Millinder, the band leader. With all this talent, the most talented of them all was a not too-well-known trumpet player by the name of Louis Armstrong. His powerful horn led this revue seven nights a week, without a conductor. There were no Jazz critics or columnists to write about Louie's magnificent playing. Word of mouth travelled from coast to coast. Louis became the most talked about musician in the country. No one used the word 'Jazz' to define Louie's playing; everybody knew he was hearing a true master. After the floor show the band would play a short dance set. They would take a stock-arrangement of some Broadway show tune that Louie loved to play (one in particular was Noel Coward's "Poor Little Rich Girl") and play the introduction, verse and chorus as it was written, down to the coda and then Louie would play twenty or more improvised choruses, always to an exciting climax! I have *never* heard anything like it, nor do I expect I shall ever hear anything to equal it again. After prohibition ended Joe Glaser became Louie's manager. Louie's horn made Glaser a millionaire.

A PUPIL WELL TAUGHT

In the days in Chicago, before Louis Armstrong became world famous, he spent a great deal of time walking the streets of his neighborhood on the southside. Louis was very friendly, and kind to everyone, especially pan-handlers.

One afternoon, as he strolled along 35th Street, he noticed a small crowd gathered around two street musicians. He stopped to listen and much to his delight, the trumpet player was playing Louis' improvised chorus of "Struttin With Some Barbecue." At the finish of the number, Louis walked over to the street musicians and said,

"Man . . . you're playing that *too slow!*"

"How would you know?" they challenged.

"I'm Louis Armstrong . . . that's my chorus you're playing!"

The next day the street musicians had a sign next to their tin cup. The sign read . . . **"PUPILS OF LOUIS ARMSTRONG."**

OPEN HOUSE

In 1929 the great Louis Armstrong had returned from a successful tour of the country. He had not become famous yet, but, of course, every musician in the world had heard his recordings. He was to open at a nightclub in Chicago called the "My Cellar" and he held his rehearsals in his house in the most impoverished section of the southside. I called him and asked if I could attend his rehearsal and he very graciously invited me to come. Now it was a warm summer day and all the doors and windows in the house were open. The "King" had come home and all of

16

the people in the neighborhood heard about the rehearsal. When I arrived at his home it was jammed with people Louis had never seen before. As soon as he saw me, he took me aside and whispered, "Watch your pockets."

REX WRITES TO LOUIE

I have just finished reading Rex Stewart's "Jazz Masters of the Thirties." I was reminded of my first meeting with Rex. He was about 18 years of age, and I was 19. We were playing at the Graystone Ballroom in Detroit, Michigan, Rex, with Fletcher Henderson, and I with the Chicagoans.

I had known Louis Armstrong for about three years. When Rex discovered this, he was after me every night to tell him about his idol. On our closing night of the engagement, Rex handed me a note to give to Louis. There was no envelope. It was just a folded piece of paper. I couldn't resist reading it. It read, "Dear Rubber-Lips: You are my idol. God Bless you and keep swinging. Your boy, Rex."

DEATH GOES TO A PARTY

One of the most ludicrous events of the year was the funeral of the great Louis Armstrong. There he lay, entertaining in death, as he had in life. People who never knew him, and as a matter of fact, put him down as an "Uncle Tom," were all there cashing in on the television coverage. I didn't go to Louis' funeral; I'm famous enough. Why has death always been so commercial?

THE MAN WHO INVENTED THE ZOOT SUIT

Josh Billings was a high school friend, one of the most unique people I've known. His mother was fifty and his father was fifty-five years of age when Josh was born. When his mother announced to her husband that she was pregnant, her husband reacted with shock and said, "Molly! What have I done to make you unfaithful to me?" Josh's parents were doctors who had very little time for anything as strange as a child in their own home, so Josh was actually raised by the maid, a big black lady, who had been with the doctors for years. Josh loved the music of the black man as much as we did. Whenever the question of race came up, Josh used to say, "I don't know if I have any black blood in me, but I certainly have a lot of black milk in me." Since his parents paid little attention to him, he was left to do whatever he wished. He was a good painter (I think that he identified with the French impressionists) and he loved to read, especially the books that were suppressed. He dressed very smartly and was always drawing sketches of well-dressed men. One day he called to tell me that he had designed a suit that he thought might change the style of men's dress completely. The trousers were high peg-top, full in the legs and tapered down to very narrow, cuffless bottoms. The jacket was long, with wide lapels and one button, which was not worn buttoned, and there was a tight vest. Although the suit was a departure from what we were wearing, it was not extreme. In fact, it was rather smart. My brother, Dave Tough, Josh, Jim Lanigan, Jimmy and Dick McPartland and I had suits of this design made immediately. This was in 1927, and I do not recall that our contemporaries paid much attention to our dress. We were musicians, and I suppose they expected anything of us. After about a year, what with our ideas changing many times, we changed to wearing something more conservative.

Now a very strange thing happened; about 1932 we were beginning to see poorly dressed men (I mean poorly dressed regarding taste) wearing what I'd call a satirical version of Josh's suit. The jackets were extremely long, showing very little leg, and the trouser bottoms were ridiculously narrow. There was a hat worn with this ensemble that resembled the Hollywood idea of a gangster. In fact, the clothes worn in the Broadway production of "Guys and Dolls" were exactly the style I speak of. It seems incredible to me that this could have happened, but I've checked on this with many people who remember that era, and they all agree that there was *never* a model of this suit ever advertised until, of course, the style had spread all over the world. Josh was, indeed, a unique guy.

THE GREAT BIX

People are constantly asking me about the legendary Bix Beiderbecke. Why was he always so drunk? People like to think of him as a knocked out character who was never sober. On the contrary, all of his great recordings were made when he was completely sober. Any great player will agree with me when I say that it is *impossible* to play when you're drunk. The first thing that goes wrong is your breathing and, of course, your brain doesn't function. Bix was an alcoholic but certainly no different than hundreds of thousands of other alcoholics of whom we shall never hear, simply because they are not in the limelight. If Bix had not been a player he would surely have been something great because he was a deep, talented man. I'll never forget the time I was playing with Ben Pollack at the Little Club in New York, and Bix knew that I was very interested in the theatre. John Barrymore had just returned from London with his great Shakespearean Co., and during one of the band's intermissions, Bix very excitedly came running down the stairs of the Club and yelled, "Bud, for God's sake hurry up; John Barrymore is doing Hamlet on radio!" I was an hour and a half late getting back to the band and was nearly fired that night. Incidentally, John Barrymore was terribly hammy in the movies, but I think that he was the greatest Hamlet of them all.

But to get back to Bix, I wish that people who had *only* the opportunity to hear him on records could have heard him in person. It was an unforgetable experience. The first time I heard the great Bessie Smith, Bix took me to hear her. He would go completely out of his mind and throw all of his money at her. She worked in a little place called the "Paradise Gardens" in Chicago. She opened at midnight and worked all night as a table singer. She used to come out unannounced; she would sing 30 or 40 choruses on one given song and to this day I have not heard anyone to compare with her. She was the greatest blues singer the world has ever known, and they let her die like an animal on the highway. It's possible that I might *never* have heard her in person, had it not been for Bix.

How often I've heard people say that it was a pity he lived only thirty years. His life was completely filled with creating beautiful music. From that point of view, he lived a perfect life.

BRICKTOP

I met Bricktop at her bar in Paris in 1929. Dave Tough introduced me to her. She was one of the many black entertainers who left the United States in the early part of the twentieth century, never to return. Obviously, there was a freer life in Europe for her. After her career as an entertainer came to an end (she had become very famous) she opened her bar which became the rendezvous of many famous artists, writers (Hemmingway and Fitzgerald practically lived there), musicians, actors, kings, queens, lords and ladies. Bricktop was the most sophisticated night-club hostess of her time — everybody loved her.

Dave Tough told me that the first time he met her he was playing in a club in Berlin, Germany. She walked up to the bandstand as the band was playing and yelled at Dave: "Go on back to Chicago where you belong." She and Dave had never seen one another before this meeting; nor had she ever heard of him. Jazz music brought together two creative people who became dear friends.

Bricktop *did* return to the United States recently; she was honored by the press. I hopes she writes a book — what stories she could tell!

IT HAPPENED IN CHICAGO

The jazz critics (not the musicians) have given the titles to jazz such as, "New Orleans jazz," "West Coast Jazz," "Chicago Jazz," and "Kansas City Jazz." We who know better have always thought of these categories as being ridiculous. A man could play or he couldn't no matter where he came from. There is strong argument today that jazz may *not* have come from Africa. It doesn't matter to me what its source may be; I'm only interested in music that moves me. However, I must make an exception. In the twenties, there was only one place to be and that was Chicago. No other city in the world had the talent or feeling for this music at that time. Jazz was the way of life in Chicago.

In 1928, I joined Ben Pollack's band to go to New York City. Just before leaving Chicago, I ran into Don Redmond who had played with Fletcher Henderson and McKinney's Cotton Pickers many times in New York. When I told him that I was going to New York, he said,

"Bud, you won't like it there. They don't swing."

"Do you mean to tell me that the colored musicians don't swing?", I asked.

"I mean to tell you that they don't swing, PERIOD!" he said.

Of course he wasn't talking about such masters as Willie the Lion Smith or Bix Beiderbeck. Louis Armstrong was not to take the town by storm until later. Jack Teagarten also came to New York later. James P. Johnson and Fats Waller had played in Chicago and never stopped talking about the difference between Chicago and New York. Bricktop told Dave Tough to go back to Chicago where he belonged (Why not New Orleans? Why not New York?) because Chicago was where it was happening. Later on, all the greats moved to New York because it offered more lucrative opportunities. The greatest jazz music in history had left Chicago — never to return.

CONDON'S SUITE

In the early thirties Eddie Condon was living, when he could afford it, at the Elk Hotel on 53rd St. between Broadway and Seventh Avenues in New York City. The hotel was located just above "Plunkets" the well-known speakeasy — hangout for musicians.

My brother and I called Eddie one day to ask after his health. He asked us to come over, and we asked where we should meet him, since the hotel didn't appear big enough to hold three people.

"Oh meet me in the Gangrene room," he said. After seeing Eddie's room, my brother asked,

"How much are you paying a day?"

"Fifty cents," Eddie replied.

"Oh! I think you're being overcharged," my brother said.

EDDIE CONDON

Much has been said about Eddie Condon's wit, but I think the funniest thing he ever said was at a time when everybody thought he was dying. He lay in the hospital with an infection of the pancreas and from hour to hour the doctors differed on how long he would live. One would say "I give him a day," another would say "I give him a week," and so on. But Eddie improved slowly and one day when the doctors thought he was strong enough to have visitors, I visited him and naturally asked how he was feeling and his direct reply was, "I think I'm gonna be O.K. I just heard one of the doctors say that I was on the critical list." It seems to me that too many people identify with death, they're constantly talking about it and thinking in terms of readying themselves for it. Eddie Condon died many times and has said that it's not all that great. As Robinson Jeffers, the great poet, has written, "Life and death are not serious alternatives." Musically speaking, I think that Eddie Condon has done a tremendous amount of good for Jazz. He has genuinely loved it all his life and has given hundred of musicians work through many years. He may never be forgotten.

EDDIE CONDON OPENS UP

Eddy Hubble (one of the trombone players in The World's Greatest Jazz Band), Billy Butterfield, and I were taking a taxi from La Guardia Airport to our apartments in New York City. Eddy was living in Greenwich Village, and on the way down to his place, we passed a very familiar site. It was a vacant lot that was once the address of the first Eddie Condon Club. I told Billy Butterfield and Eddy Hubble that I was one of the musicians in the band that played there on the opening night; that there was a great deal of panic around the place because the paint on the chairs, tables, and bar had not dried in time to serve the customers, who stood around as though they were at a cocktail party, waiting to be served a drink. Eddy Hubble suddenly remembered something that happened that night. He said that the first drink was sold to a minor, a young man seventeen years of age. Now the club opened at the end of 1945. Eddy is forty-three; how could he know about this, I thought. I told him that he must have been mistaken — he was too young to have been there. He snapped back at me indignantly, "I oughta know; I was the minor they sold the drink to."

CHICAGO STYLE MUSICIAN

'Horsey' Dean, a piano playing bandleader in the twenties in Chicago, was called 'Horsey' because of his voice.

He was a tough sort of guy, and one night in a saloon fight, he was shot in the neck. Miraculously he lived, but nearly lost his voice. The only sound that remained was a hoarse rasp. Immediately after leaving the hospital, he bought a pistol, which he carried with him whenever he played. He got a job playing in a road house that was a hangout for gunmen. One night as he was putting his music away, after having played his last number, a man approached the bandstand and requested a song to be played. Horsey's immediate response to the request was, "Nuttin' doin.' It's three o'clock. We're goin' home."

The man pulled a gun out of his holster and pointed it at Horsey.

"Horsey," he said, "I ain't kiddin.' Play another song."

Horsey very casually reached into his pocket, pulled his pistol out and shot the man between the eyes. Nothing was ever done about it because the gunman was at large and the police were glad to get rid of him. Horsey was acquitted on self-defense. In those days the music was *really hot in Chicago!*

A SCHOLAR OF BOP

In another part of this book, I told of having gone to Manchester, England, to play a jazz festival with Dizzy Gillespie and Buck Clayton. On the first day, we rehearsed in tents. The day was unusually hot, to say nothing of the tents. Dizzy had had a few drinks and was feeling no pain, . . . in fact, he was feeling no clothes. He rehearsed practically in the nude (apparently he was going through his "Gandhi" phase). A boy about twelve years of age, after having watched Dizzy for about two hours, came up to me and asked,

"Mr. Freeman, is this real bop, or do they wear their clothes when they play?"

Later, when I told this to Dizzy, he fell out laughing.

THE PERFECT DIVORCE

Barrett Deems, the great drummer (the funniest man I've ever met), was telling about his recent divorce. I asked him if he would be getting married again. "Oh, God no — I don't have time!" he said.

BILL DOHLER

One of the brightest, craziest and most talented saxophone players I've ever known is my old friend Bill Dohler who lives in Chicago and freelances there. Just before the Second World War, Bill and I played together in a nightclub and in those days the hours of playing ran into the morning, sometimes until 5 o'clock. Bill and I lived on the north side and many mornings after work we'd walk home through Lincoln Park . On one such morning we stopped in a bar (in Chicago some bars never closed) and got pretty drunk, and Bill said, "Let's take some peanuts up to the Zoo and feed the animals." When we arrived at the Zoo the only animals awake were the Polar and Grizzly bears. Bill put a handful of peanuts through the bars of the Polar bear's cage and the Polar ate the peanuts without touching Bill's hand, but when Bill tried this with the female Grizzly in the next cage, she nearly tore his fingers off. Luckily Bill's hand healed in a few weeks and one morning on one of his wild drunken escapades, he decided to get even with the female Grizzly, so he got one of his golf clubs, went over to the cage and struck the Grizzly over the head and as she was going down, Bill said, "Do you know that she had a guilty look on her face."

In 1942 Bill received his greetings from Uncle Sam and was so infuriated that he decided he'd do anything to stay out of the war. Now, when Bill was about ten years of age his leg was badly injured in a motorcycle accident and to this day his leg has a large dent in it. The night before he was to appear at his draft board for a physical examination he got drunk, took a hammer and banged his old injury until his leg swelled up to twice it's normal size. He then went out and bought a crutch which he wore to the draft board and surely enough they took him into the army!

As anyone who has ever taken an army physical examination knows, you go through several doctors' offices, finally ending up in the psychiatrist's office. By the time you get there, you are stark naked. This, of course, gives the doctor a tremendous advantage since he is clothed. The following is Bill's interview with the doctor.

Doctor: "Have you ever had an affair with a man?"

Bill: "No. Have you?"

Doctor: "Answer the question, and don't get smart with me."

Bill: "What was the question?"

Doctor: "Never mind. Have you ever been in jail?"

Bill: "Yes."

Doctor: "Really? What for?"

Bill: "I played for some prisoners."

Doctor: "Oh, I give up!! You're not very smart, are you?"

Bill: "Listen, if I were sitting there dressed and you were sitting here naked, you wouldn't be so damned smart."

Doctor: "Get the hell out of here!"

They took Bill into the army where he remained for four years!

THE DUEL

Bill Dohler told me a delightful story about Louis Armstrong.

Bill and Louie were sitting in a club, listening to a jazz group when in walked Jabbo Smith, the trumpet player. Jabbo had been making quite a name for himself as a possible threat to Louie's hegemony. Louie listened to Jabbo for about an hour and then decided he had heard about enough. He took his horn out of a small leather bag, turned to Bill Dohler and said, "You don't know these people. I gotta defend myself." After Louie finished playing, he received a standing ovation.

SIBLING RIVALRY

The Dorsey brothers were not Jazz musicians, but I've never known any musicians who loved to play more than they. They came out of an era of the dance bands, but they could easily have played in the symphony — so well had they been trained in their youth. Their father was a fine music teacher who, perhaps, not realizing that he favored one son over the other, caused a love-hate relationship between them that was never to end. I knew them all of my life and I was forever trying to break up fist fights between them. They tried to work together many times, but finally came to the realization that they could no longer do it, and so after one last bout they separated.

Of course, they made a million dollars as individual band leaders, but I'm certain that they never stopped competing with each other. The last fight they were ever to have, took place at Tommy's opening at the 'Asor Roof' in New York. Tommy had added violins to his band and Jimmy, who had come to his brother's opening night, danced up to him and said, "Oh, you had to add fiddles to make it, eh." Upon hearing this Tommy jumped off the bandstand and they punched each other all over the place. It was the best show in town. (I might add that there was an unknown singer in the band by the name of Frank Sinatra.)

I truly believe that after Tommy died, Jimmy's challenge in life died also, no matter what the final diagnosis of his illness. Immediately after Tommy died, Jackie Gleason turned his television show of that week into a memorial for him. I was asked to do the show and all that Jimmy Dorsey could talk about was his brother. He died a few months later.

TOMMY DORSEY

Tommy Dorsey loved anyone who played Jazz. He was a pretty good drinker before he organized his band, but realized that he couldn't make it that way, so he gave it up. Now, interestingly enough, he had a feeling and respect for heavy drinkers, if they were good players. One night at the Commodore Hotel in New York City, Bunny Berigan, the famous trumpet player, got stoned sitting sprawled on the bandstand; his music was strewn all over the place. Tommy didn't seem to mind very much but his manager at seeing Bunny so drunk yelled,

"Why don't you fire that sonofabitch."

Tommy yelled back, "I can't fire him. He plays too good."

MAX FARLEY

The first reed player to understand the usage of the vibrato was Max Farley. Max played oboe, flute, clarinet, English horn, and saxophone. He played them beautifully. About fifty years ago the musicians playing reed instruments either played with no vibrato or with a wide vibrato. Max changed all that. He made the saxophone a thing of beauty. He was never one to accept a compliment; he always used to say, "Isn't that the way it's supposed to be played?" Max had a problem; he loved music, but he hated the music business. He also loved to drink. Paul Whiteman once said of Max, "I never saw him when he was sober, but I never heard him make a mistake." Max played oboe in many Broadway shows. A few that I remember were: "Roberta," "Strike Up The Band," and "Girl Crazy." He used to spike a bottle of coca cola with gin, and flatten two straws at the end; in the dark of the orchestra pit, they could conceivably look like an oboe to the conductor, who was usually drunk anyway. Max would then put the bottle of spiked coke in his handkerchief pocket and at every break in the music he would take a sip from the straws, making it look as though he were playing the oboe. He was the best reed player of his time, and he couldn't have cared less.

MUSIC INSTRUCTIONS

Marcus Foster, the Boston drummer, had admired Lester Young all of his life. His idol finally appeared as a soloist at 'Storyville' and Marcus had the rhythm section. Just before playing the first number, Marcus asked Lester how he would like the drums played behind him. Lester's classic answer was, "Just go tiddy-voo."

GEORGE GUINLE

In 1970, we, 'The World's Greatest Jazz Band,' toured Brazil. On our first night in Rio, I looked into the audience and saw my old friend George Guinle sitting in the first row. George had taken the first three rows in the theatre for his closest friends. He is one of the richest men in the world, probably the richest in Brazil, and he loves Jazz music. At the end of the concert George came back stage and invited the band to his luxurious apartment on the Copacabana; he had arranged a supper for us. When we arrived at his home we were enthusiastically greeted by his friends. We were wined, dined, feted, and lionized as though we were ambassadors. George played many of our old recordings — recordings we had made as individual soloists during the big band era. After supper he signaled two butlers. They bowed politely and went into another room. When they returned they were carrying a set of drums between them. They were dressèd in summer formal — Tuxedo trousers, white vests, white shirts with black bow ties, patent leather pumps, and white gloves. Their faces expressed seriousness and embarrassment, as if to say, "What will 'Senor' think of next." George then put on one of his favorite records and played along with it until the end. His friends politely applauded and then his nephew came over to me and asked, "Mr. Freeman, do you think my uncle is a little strange?" I reminded him that most of us started our lives as drummers — some of us grew out of it. He seemed to be satisfied with my explanation.

EARL AND DUKE

On a tour of Europe several years ago, Earl Hines, the pianist, and I were playing in a band called, "Jazz of the Swing Era." Earl Hines has been known for many years as FATHA HINES. As we entered the elevator of our hotel in Copenhagen, Denmark, we bumped into Duke Ellington, who was coming out. Duke, upon seeing Earl Hines cried, "FATHA." Earl, upon seeing Duke, cried, "Motha."

BENNY GOODMAN

When I was fifteen years old and had just got my first long pants suit, I went to a street dance. These dances took place, of course, in the summer; a block was roped off and a bandstand was set up in the middle of the block. Jimmy McPartland had already begun to play professionally and invited me to the dance. There was a kid in the band playing the clarinet; he was no more than thirteen years of age. He played the clarinet so beautifully! — It was not to be believed. He had the technique of a master and a beautiful sound to go with it! His name was Benny Goodman. He was a very pleasant little guy, who hadn't the faintest idea of the extraordinary talent he possessed.

I was not to have the good fortune to play with him until I joined the Ben Pollack band in 1928. Benny was always very pleasant and encouraging to me; it was quite a thrill sitting next to this master every night. One night at the 'Little Club' in New York, Ben Pollack suggested that we have a jam session on the "Blues." He asked me to play the clarinet (I could imitate Jimmy Noone, the great New Orleans clarinet player) and Benny Goodman played my tenor saxophone. I was amazed when I heard Benny play the tenor. He had the best sound I have ever heard, before or since. There has never been anyone like him. I don't mean to imply that he's a creative player; but he is certainly a masterful player.

BOB HAGGART

I have known so many fine musicians, that to pick out one as being the absolute best would be impossible. If I could do this, then Bob Haggart would certainly be the man. He is an excellent bass player, a fine arranger, and a very creative composer. Unlike many arrangers, he seems to treat the piece of music he is arranging as an original composition. His compositions, "What's New" and "Rampart Street Parade" have held up for more than twenty-five years, and are to me as fresh today as they were at their birth. At the end of the "Big Band Era" he was faced with having to make a decision — as were hundreds of other musicians. Radio and television had now become the thing. If a musician could do this sort of work, which meant reading music at sight, he found himself in a very lucrative position. In addition to this, he could make a home for himself in whatever city he chose to work. Bob made his decision. He stayed in New York (at that time the top city in the world for this kind of work) and played on many of the biggest radio and television shows. Since this kind of work afforded not very much opportunity to play Jazz, his favorite music, he took advantage of every chance he had to play in jam sessions and recording dates. His true dedication to music has given him a name that may never die.

CONVERSATION WITH THE HAWK

A short time before Coleman Hawkins died, I invited him to my apartment for a drink; he stayed all day. He especially liked the taste of vodka and grapefruit juice, and after a few hours we drank a quart of vodka. We talked about our early days (I had known him for forty-five years) and I asked him about a record he made with Mamie Smith and her 'Jazz Hounds.' I suggested that he had to be ninety years old, because I was fifteen when I heard it. He laughed and said, "Man, I made that record when I was nine years old." Our conversation turned to a serious discussion of music; I asked him why, after all these years of playing, our styles were still in demand. My question seemed to sober him and his answer was something that the young player might find to be very instructive: "We are in demand *today* because we knew our horns when we were *young*."

HARRY THE HIPSTER

The only jazz musician ever known to have given a dimension of humor to drug addiction was the pianist-entertainer, Harry the Hipster. All of the songs that he sang led his audience to believe that getting "high" could be a lot of fun. Of course, he was a fine pianist who preferred to have fun with his music. Had he not been an entertainer, he could easily have succeeded as a serious pianist, but I'm glad that he did what he did; he was truly a very funny man. He was a very handsome guy — one of the first in the Twentieth Century to wear long hair, but instead of letting it grow wild as is the fashion today, he pomaded it straight back, giving him the appearance of something resembling a white parrot. He did all of his playing standing up facing his audience, never once looking at the keyboard. On cue, a waiter would bring him a large glass of bourbon and coke, which Harry would mix with aspirin, then drink it down in one swallow. A la Dr. Jekyll and Mr. Hyde, he transformed himself into readiness to play and sing. All of his material was based on addiction of one form or another. Some of his hilarious verses were: "Some cats stay brown all year round. I stay green all year-ene." "Get your juices from the Deuces" (referring to the 3 Deuces — the jazz spot on 52nd Street). My favorite verse was the satire on the song, "La Cucaracha": "La Marijuana, La Marijuana, she is the one for me."

In 1948, I opened at the "Blue Note" in Chicago; the engagement was for a month. I was supposed to alternate with Harry the Hipster, but he showed up a day late and appeared just one night. I have not seen him since. I hope that he sees this book. I'd like to know where he's playing.

ROGER WOLFE KAHN

In 1933 I played with Roger Wolfe Kahn and his orchestra. Our first job was at the old 'Claremont' restaurant up on Riverside Drive. We played outdoors during the month of July, and every time it rained we went home. This presented a financial problem to the owners of the restaurant, especially since the band had a very high payroll. Now Roger was the son of the financier Otto Kahn, and everytime it rained, the owners would ask Roger to buy the place. Roger's refusal to do so gave the owners the excuse they needed to fire the band.

The last night we played there, I had some fun with one of the customers, a lady who kept calling me waiter everytime I passed her table. Before we were to play our last set, I walked over to the lady and asked what I could do for her. She snapped at me and demanded that I bring her steak. I asked the headwaiter if he would allow me to bring a steak to her, and he agreed because he thought there could be no harm in having a little fun with this woman who was sort of a pest anyway. We had a half-hour intermission, which gave me just enough time to serve the steak and get to the bandstand. I served the steak with the help of the bus-boy and then casually walked to the bandstand, picked up my horn and started to play. When the woman saw this she walked over to me and said, "Oh, you play the saxophone too — you don't *look* like a musician."

Roger Wolfe Kahn was a fine guy and an excellent musician, but his great wealth became an obstacle to our getting work. He wasn't interested in owning any restaurants — we disbanded!

THE PAINTER DIDN'T MEAN ANY HARM

Adolph Hitler was on the air so often that people who had short-wave sets were picking him up all over the world. In fact, they could get nothing else.

Maxie Kaminsky, the famous trumpet player, understood German and after hearing Hitler for the first time, called me to say,

31

"Gee, Bud, I just picked up Hitler on short-wave."
"Really, what did he say," I asked.
"Oh nothing personal," said Maxie.

JIM LANIGAN, BASSIST

Jim Lanigan, the fine bass player with the 'Austin High Gang' and later with the Chicago Symphony, was the brother-in-law of the McPartland brothers, Jimmy, the cornet player, and Dick, the guitarist. Jim loved to play, but the thought of going on the road was too much for him. He was a home-body. He decided to study for the symphony and eventually joined the Chicago Symphony Orchestra. About the same time that he joined the symphony, I joined Ben Pollack's band and left Chicago to work in New York. We of the Jazz world were very proud of our friend who had the musicianship to play in the Symphony, never realizing that there could be tremendous problems there also. In 1937 the Chicago Orchestra played a guest concert at Carnegie Hall in New York City. Frederick Stock was the conductor and I remember sitting just behind the great Toscanini who had come to see his old friend. After the concert I went backstage to see Jim, to congratulate him. His immediate response was, "Oh Bud, it's the worst kind of work. As you know we have several bassists in the orchestra and everytime one of them makes a mistake, we all get blamed."

GERALD LASCELLES

Gerald Lascelles, cousin of the Queen of Britain, nephew of the late Duke of Windsor, has been a Jazz fan since he was a boy. I met him fifteen years ago and was very surprised to find that he knew more about the recordings I had made than I do. At his home, 'Ft. Belvedere,' in London, he has entertained hundreds of Jazz musicians for vears. He is a gracious, unassuming gentleman who truly loves music. His wife, a former actress, is a charming lovely person who possesses a marvelous sense of humor. During a tour of Great Britain several years ago, I received an invitation to dine with them at the Fort. As we were having cocktails, Gerald's wife said, "You know, Mr. Freeman, we have nothing but Royalty here. We have the Duke of Ellington, the Count of Basie, and Willie, the lion heart, Smith." I never realized how much Gerald idolized Jazz musicians until just recently when he was mistaken for Yank Lawson (he and Yank resemble each other) backstage at a theatre in London. A man slapped him on the back and asked,

"How about your autograph, Yank." Gerald actually was thrilled and said,

"How wonderful it must be to be famous."

Jazz music is deeply indebted to him.

HE COULD QUIT ANYTIME HE LIKED

When Wingy Manone, the famous trumpet player from New Orleans, was asked if he thought marijuana was habit forming, he replied, "I've been smokin' it for forty years — I *know* it aint' habit formin'."

MEZZ

The first time I saw Milton Mesirow, he was playing in a Chinese restaurant in Chicago. I was very impressed with his enthusiasm for the black man's music. He was the first white man I had ever met who truly understood the language and thinking of the black man. He was certainly one of the first to see that the black man refused to be brainwashed into believing the things the white man had believed since the beginning of time. Mezz was not a talented man, but he had a deeper feeling for the black man's music than anyone I had ever met. He was very helpful to me in the first year I played — always trying to convince me that I had an original style of playing and that I felt the music very deeply. Mezz was the first man to organize a black and white band long before John Hammond gave the idea to Benny Goodman. I am convinced that Mezz actually believed he was a black man. He was one of the most extraordinary men I have ever met. Surely he must have convinced many blacks that white people are not all bad.

HENRY MORGAN

I have never been able to remember people's names; especially when called upon to make any introductions. I remember introducing my uncle to someone; my uncle had the same name as I, but I couldn't remember it.

33

In 1933 I met a young man by the name of Henry Van something or other. He was later to become famous, and is now known as Henry Morgan. Everytime I met him, I had to ask him his name. He seemed not to be upset about this, but I always felt embarrassed. I was not to see Henry again until after the war. As I was passing Hurley's Bar and Grill on my way over to NBC one day, a man came running out of the bar. He was the famous Henry Morgan. He grabbed me by the shoulders and yelled, "Now, you son of a bitch, do you remember my name?"

AN ORIGINAL POINT OF VIEW

Benny Morton, the trombone player, is one of the most gracious men I have ever met. One day, at lunch, I asked him how he managed to stay so relaxed all the time. He smiled and said, "Well, you see, Bud, I don't have the stamina to fight what the world is really like."

JIMMY McPARTLAND

Although Dave Tough had the biggest musical influence on me, Jimmy McPartland helped me more than anyone. He was the first person to take an interest in me, as having some sort of talent. When my father and I quarreled about my not making some sort of a living, Jimmy took me into his home and supported me until I played my first job. This was not the only time. Later in New York, Jimmy took me and Dave Tough into his apartment and fed us until we got work. He was the most generous friend a man could have. Jimmy idolized Bix, and to this day his sound is more like Bix than any other player. The last time I heard him, he was playing better than ever. He has been playing fifty years at this writing, and when the Jazz histories are written for posterity, his name will appear on many pages.

RAY NOBLE

In 1934, Ray Noble, his manager, and Al Bowlly the singer, came over to the United States to work and, of course, to organize an American band. Some labor law existed at that time which did not allow Ray to bring his

British band into the States. The Dorsey Brothers were helpful in suggesting the best players in New York and auditions and rehearsals were held to determine what musicians would be hired. Now Ray Noble was an English gentleman — a graduate of Cambridge — who was not aware that English and American were two different languages. I had, since my childhood, seen many British plays, and was very familiar with this strange language. It was only natural that I be called upon to interpret for the band. As incredible as it may seem, the men did not understand a word that Ray uttered. I, of course, enjoyed it all no end! As the band became more organized, what with recording and playing club dates, we were signed to play the "Coty Hour." On the night of the band's debut, the elevator operators struck all over town. The "Coty Hour" was scheduled to start at 8:30 p. m. Ray Noble lived on the 33rd floor of a very posh apartment hotel in Central Park South. He walked down the 33 flights and appeared, impeccably dressed, in white tie and tails, one minute before we went on the air. He seemed not in the least upset, and went on to direct the band as though what had happened were an every day occurrence. I had never seen anyone quite like him. He used to say to me, "Buddy, you understand me. Will you tell the fellas what I mean?" One night I forgot to tell the fellas what he meant and, of course, all hell brook lose! "Cahn't you play the bloody thing?" he screamed. Up to this time Ray had been a perfect gentleman, but with the language barrier, it was just a bit much for him. Since the inception of the band there were many changes in personnel, but the musicians who were to become famous were: Toots Mondello, saxophone and flute; Johnny Mince, clarinet; Will Bradley, trombone; Glen Miller, trombone; Claude Thornhill, piano; Pee Wee Irwin, trumpet; George Van Epps, guitar; and Charlie Spivak, trumpet.

After having played the Coty Hour for several months, it seemed a natural occurrence to show up every Tuesday for the show's rehearsal. On one such rehearsal day, one of the musicians didn't show up. It appeared that he was having an affair with a married woman whose husband came home unexpectedly. The frantic woman locked her lover in a closet where he lay for eleven hours. After he luckily escaped without a broken bone, he called the studio and announced that he didn't know there was a rehearsal. Upon hearing this, Ray Noble went into a rage and screamed, "Didn't know my ahss!" Now the musicians had never heard the word 'ass' used with a broad 'a' before — they rolled on the floor laughing, and I can't remember to this day what ever happened to the lover. I remained with the band for eighteen months and then joined Tommy Dorsey's band. Several of the key men had found what they felt to be better offers and left the band one by one. Glen Miller, who was one of the last big names to leave, got drunk one night and said, "Ray, if you're not careful, they're going to be saying, "Here come the British with a bad, bad band.'" With all due respect to Ray Noble, he was a fine musician and a gentleman — a rare thing in the music business.

FREDDY PFAFF

We were playing in Orlando, Florida for two days. There's a night club-restaurant there called 'Monte's.' It is one of the finest places to play in the country. One of our fans who was sitting at a table near the bandstand called out to Bob Haggart and Yank Lawson. They went over to see him and were joyously surprised. Yank Lawson called me over to the table and said, "Bud, this is Freddy Pfaff, one of the greatest tuba players of all time!!!"

Freddy lives in Orlando where he played with the Florida symphony. He just retired from the orchestra because he doesn't want to travel anymore. He's eighty-four years of age, but his mind is very sharp. He had played with John Philip Sousa over sixty years ago.

He told us a delightful story about the conductor of the Florida symphony. The orchestra was rehearsing "The Stars and Stripes Forever." The arranger had written the piccolo part for the tuba. It was to be played at a very rapid tempo. Freddy said that it was almost impossible to play on tuba. The conductor stopped the orchestra and in sympathy with Freddy said, "Do you know that if I had written that, I wouldn't have written it?"

MY CRAZY DRUMMER

I think that we tend to exaggerate when we accuse

people of being crazy or insane, but I did actually have a drummer in my group who was genuinely crazy. I could never get him to come to work on time, and night after night I'd repeat that the hours we worked were the same every night excepting on Saturdays we started an hour earlier. After my yelling at him one night he became very indignant and yelled back, "I know man, the hours are the same, except Saturday which has thirty days." One day two men in white suits came and took him away.

A similar kind of guy was a well known musician by the name of Jack Purvis, who was married seven times and never divorced once. He, of course, was sent to prison for a long time and I think that he became the director of a band at San Quentin. He tried to commit suicide one night in his apartment by turning on the gas. It was a very cold February night and as they were carrying him out on a stretcher, he came to and screamed, "For Christ's sake cover up my feet, do you want me to catch pneumonia and die?"

STREET SCENE

Just after the Second World War, I saw Don Redmond standing on the corner of 55th Street and Seventh Avenue in New York City. I had not seen him in twenty years. He had been living in France. We talked about the early days (many of our old friends had died) and how different everything seemed. Suddenly, other friends whom we had not seen in a long time gathered around to say, "hello." After several minutes, there were at least 25 people milling around. To anyone who wasn't acquainted with us, we must have given the impression that we were creating a disturbance. Surely enough, a policeman came running over and ordered us to break it up and move on. As we were saying "good-bye," Don said, "It's even against the law to say 'hello.'"

PEE WEE

I was not to find that Pee Wee Russell, the famous Jazz clarinet player, was very bright and articulate until the end of his life. Pee Wee had begun to drink at about the age of fourteen and was extremely nervous and it was almost impossible to carry on a conversation of any rapport with him. He was a kind and generous man and certainly the most unique player of his time. Wherever we played around the world Pee Wee was famous. I don't think that other musicians appreciated Pee Wee's playing because they were looking for a facility that is generally expected of a good player, but I think that Pee Wee had more to say in his playing than all the technicians put together. About a year before he died he took up painting and, of course, when he painted he was absolutely sober. One day I called him to ask about his new hobby and he spoke so clearly that I thought I had the wrong number. I'd say that Pee Wee's style of painting was somewhat after the fashion of Juan Miro. The whole world seemed to know about it. I took it upon myself to act as his art agent and was amazed to find that people were willing to pay whatever I thought was reasonable to ask. The paintings that I sold were sold for not less than $700.00, and for the last two paintings I received $3,000.00. Pee Wee called to thank me and died four days later. He painted about fifty things, all of which were sold in no time at all. I asked my wife one day what she thought of Pee Wee's playing, and she said, "He sounds like a wild bird." When people asked about Pee Wee's painting, I simply explained that I thought it was a transference of talent and intelligence into another idiom. There'll never be another Pee Wee.

THE BLACK TIE

After Pee Wee Russell had been painting about six months, calls for his paintings came in from all over the country. Since I had been acting as his art agent, many of the calls came to me. One day I received a call from Pee Wee's wife, Mary, informing me that the Australian Ambassador had heard of Pee Wee's painting and was interested in presenting his work in an art show along with several Australian and New Zealand painters. The affair would be strictly black tie, and it would be held in Washington, D.C. Mary said that Pee Wee didn't want to go. I, of course, was very excited, realizing that this show could launch Pee Wee into becoming a painter of world renown. I called him to insist that he go, and his incredible reaction was,

"But, Bud, I don't have a black tie."

"Well get one for Christsake," I screamed.

He didn't go to Washington; after I calmed down it dawned on me that Pee Wee didn't really think that he was a painter . . . he could have fooled the Australian Ambassador.

HE LOVED TO LIVE

Ernie Anderson, advisor to Ingmar Bergman and John Houston, told me that the first time he heard of Pee Wee Russell, Pee Wee was dying. Pee Wee was to go on living through many serious illnesses since then.

Many people have asked me how Pee Wee managed to survive. I couldn't resist filching a line from Lao-Tzu, the Chinese sage. "He had no death to die."

JIMMY RUSHING

The late Jimmy Rushing, the famous blues singer, was named by his close friends "Mr. Five by Five." He actually was five-feet, five-inches tall and weighed three hundred pounds.

I had the pleasure of playing a concert tour with him in New Zealand. The first town was Aukland. We had reservations at a lovely hotel, but the rooms were very small. Jimmy couldn't get into his room, and when the bell-hop suggested he try going in side ways, Jimmy responded with: "But you don't understand, man. I'm the same size all around!"

JACK TEAGARDEN

In 1928 I was playing with Ben Pollack at the 'Little Club' in New York City. About 3 o'clock one morning I received a call from Pee Wee Russell, the clarinet player.

"Bud, get dressed in a hurry and come over to Mike's on 53rd St. Jack Teagarden, the best trombone player in the world, just blew into town from Oklahoma City and he wants to meet you, and I asked him to bring his horn."

Mike's was a speakeasy and hangout for musicians, writers and show people. It never closed. I got there as soon as I could and found Pee Wee at the bar.

"Wait'll you hear this guy play, you won't believe it," he

said. A few minutes later in walked Jack with his horn; it was in a corduroy bag. He wore a small cap with a button on top, a Norfolk suit with trousers halfway up his legs and suede shoes. He took his horn out and played, with no accompaniment, some of the most beautiful music I've ever heard. "Clothes don't always make the man," I thought. He had no job. He had just come to New York to look for work. A man of his talent wasn't going to be out of work very long. Now Glen Miller had just announced that he was leaving the Pollack band and, of course, upon hearing this I couldn't wait to tell Pollack about Jack. Pollack, who was a fine drummer, heard Jack play for five minutes and hired him. In the band were Benny Goodman and Jimmy McPartland, who flipped when they heard Jack. Jack's playing completely changed the style of the band. Benny Goodman, up to the time of hearing Jack, had not played much melody. He became a strong melodic player. I'm certain that this influence contributed strongly to Benny's greatness. I don't know what happened to Benny Goodman to make him so disliked. I only know that as a young man he was one of the finest men I'd ever known — and certainly a fine artist. Jack and I became close friends. I had been reading Shakespeare a great deal of the time and Jack used to break up laughing at me. He'd ask,

"How can a low-down, gut-bucket saxophone player like you understand Shakespeare?"

"I don't know whether I want to be an actor or a musician," I used to say.

"Well, why don't you be both?" he'd suggest. I became both.

I was saddened by the news of his death. He lived only to play his horn. He was a great artist!

TEAGARDEN AND THE KING OF SIAM

Several years ago, the King of Thailand visited the United States. His Highness is a saxophone player, a composer, and a rabid jazz fan. He was greeted by the top executives of the State Department who were eager to please him. They had planned a Siamese setting for him thinking that this would be the proper manner to honor so distinguished a guest. He immediately declined saying that he had come to the United States to hear some jazz music and that he wasn't in the least interested in hearing about his great grandfather and all his women. The first musician he asked for was Jack Teagarden, the famous trombone player. Did anybody know where Jack was playing and how soon could they find out? When finally Jack and the King met, the King treated Jack as though he, Jack, were the King.

"How does one address a King?" Jack asked.

"You call me Mr. Saxophone and I'll call you Mr. Trombone," said the King.

Jack told me later that the King was a good saxophone player. Once again, jazz plays the part of diplomat.

DAVE TOUGH

Dave Tough, the great drummer, was a most extraordinary person in that he not only played the drums better than anyone in the world but was highly intellectual. One day in high school, he asked me if I'd like to see an exhibit of Cezanne's work then being shown at the Chicago Art Institute. As I recall, we were about fifteen years of age. Upon seeing Cezanne's paintings for the first time, I said that I wished I could say something about this magnificent work. Dave replied that that was the best thing I could ever say about it. Dave was the brightest and most humorous man I have ever known. One of the first jobs he played was in a band whose leader had a nymphomanical wife. One day, the leader walked into his room and found his wife and Dave in bed together. Dave sat up and said: "Thank God it's you, Jim."

THE BROADMINDED CUCKOLD

Dave Tough and his first wife went to Europe where Dave played in the nightclubs of Berlin and Paris for three years. They had been inseparable until he discovered that she was having an affair with the piano player in the band. Dave left her and returned to New York. I had a small apartment and invited him to stay with me until he found work. After a couple of months had passed, his unfaithful wife returned to New York and called me asking if I had seen him. I asked him if he wanted to see her and he said that he'd like to spend a day with her in my apartment.

41

I agreed and left. I stayed away for two days. When I returned she was gone.

"What do you think of your wife now?" I asked.

"I don't like her! — she cheated on the piano player," he replied.

JOE VENUTI

Hundreds of anecdotes have been told about the famous violinist, but I always found Joe to be funniest when he was serious. About two years ago he alternated with our band at the Roosevelt Hotel in New York. I had not seen him in many years and in the course of our conversation, I asked about his mother, father and brothers. He said that his mother and father had passed away but that they had lived to be well over a hundred years of age. I then asked about his brothers and he said that they were ninety-two years old.

"Where are they?" I asked.

"In the hospital," he said.

"What's the matter with them?" I asked.

"Oh, they gotta cold," he said.

THE TUBA

Joe Venuti was holding a rehearsal one day on Forty-Eight Street and as he looked out the window, he saw a man carrying a gigantic tuba. He rushed downstairs to stop the man before he disappeared, and made him an offer to join his band.

"I'll give you a hundred dollars a week." The man was so taken aback that he could say nothing. "I'll give you $150.00 a week," Joe offered, but still no answer. "I'll give you $175.00 a week and that's my last offer."

The man finally broke in and said, "But, you don't understand sir, I don't play the tuba, I am delivering it."

AIN'T MISBEHAVIN'

In the early thirties I had the good fortune to know the great Fats Waller, who was considered by his contemporaries to be the best Jazz pianist alive. Fats was a very warm, generous, kind man and a dear friend. He was always playing the piano, his true love, whether he was employed or not.

One morning after having been out all night visiting other musicians in Harlem, Fats invited me to his apartment for breakfast. Waiting for the coffee pot to perk, he ran to the piano and asked how I liked a phrase that had just come into his mind. He completely forgot about the coffee and went on to develop the phrase, which became the Jazz classic "Ain't Misbehavin'." Fats had a dear friend by the name of Andy Razaf, a poet and lyricist, who was a graduate of Oxford University. Andy happened on that morning to call Fats and Fats played the song for him over the phone. Andy said, "Hold everything, I have the title." He hurried over to the apartment, listened to the song a few times and there in less than an hour wrote the words to one of the all-time classics.

Fats was spared any kind of suffering that comes with death. One night on a train he said goodnight to his manager, went to his berth, fell asleep and never woke up. When I listen to his records today, I feel his presence very strongly. His music will live forever.

PAUL WHITEMAN

Paul Whiteman was called the "King of Jazz." Of course, it was ridiculous to have given him this title since his band was purely a dance-band. But he did admire Jazz musicians and used them for years. Bix was the old man's favorite — he was treated with more respect than any musician in the band. Jack and Charlie Teagarden, George Wettling and Frank Trambaur became Paul's favorites later on.

I joined the band on a recording date in New York. It was a big band, about twenty-five men. Paul kept calling me "Jim" — we had not met before — and finally Jack Teagarden said,

"Hey Pops, his name isn't Jim — that's Bud Freeman."

Paul Whiteman looked surprised and said, "Oh! are you Bud Freeman? I heard you were coming with the band." I stayed with the band for a short period. Paul treated me beautifully.

NICOL WILLIAMSON

I've just finished reading Kenneth Tynan's profile of Nicol Williamson in the "New Yorker." The article is well written, but I cannot agree with Tynan's picture of Nicol.

We were invited to play at the White House and Nicol had very little time to prepare for the tremendous amount of material he had to remember. I played at all the rehearsals; they were tedious and difficult, and I didn't have to remember anything.

Nicol Williamson is one of the finest men I've ever met; he's unselfish, charming, kind, and considerate. I admit that I could be prejudiced, because he loves musicians; all through the rehearsals he was concerned for them, sending out for coffee, drinks, and food. If Nicol's reputation is that he can be temperamental and difficult, he must have changed suddenly, because I did not see any of this in him. He gave the White House and its guests the party of the year. Isn't it interesting that a Scottish actor could get the World's Greatest Jazz Band into the White House?

LESTER YOUNG

Lester Young, the great tenor man, was truly one of the funniest men I've ever had the pleasure to know. He was not only a very creative player, but he influenced his whole environment. The given, accepted way of playing the tenor at that time was "The Big Sound." Lester came along with a small round sound that completely took over the world. He was playing down South on a one-nighter tour in the late thirties with some of his close friends and they got sort of stranded in a small town, because they missed their train. Now the only way they could make their next gig was by taking a bus, so they hailed one that was going their way. The white bus driver didn't want to take them, so they stood in the way of the bus until he had to. He ordered them to the back of the bus and as the bus took off, Lester called out, "Drive carefully baby, drive carefully."

After Lester had left Count Basie and I had left Benny Goodman to become soloists in the Jazz field, I met him many times on concert stages and in night-clubs. One day I asked him to listen to a recording I had made of a tune called "Three Little Words." He seemed to like it very much and said, "It's a bitch." I was not to see him again until seventeen years later. We greeted each other with the usual "how have you been?" and then he said, "that three little words was a bitch."

44

JAZZ CAME FROM EVERYWHERE

One of the most popular current television shows is the "Dick Cavett Show." It is one of my favorite television shows because its guests are so interesting. Just recently Mary Lou Williams, the Jazz pianist and composer, appeared on the show. I had never heard her speak, and was delightfully surprised to hear that she had a great deal to say about Jazz music. I wrote down a few of the most interesting things she had to say:

"Jazz is important and should be played in all churches . . . Jazz, born out of suffering of the American black man, came from Africa . . . It is the greatest art in the world and everyone is trying to take credit for it . . . New Orleans just happened to be the home of many blacks . . . Jazz music was put here for everyone to play — the blacks just have a feeling for their suffering . . ."

Mary Lou Williams also stated that Jazz came from everywhere. Many players left New Orleans because they couldn't make a living there. If I were to list all of the great Jazz musicians who didn't come from New Orleans, I'd need an encyclopedia. Here are some of the greats *not* from New Orleans: Duke Ellington, Coleman Hawkins — 'Art Tatum' — Lester Young — Stan Getz — Earl Hines — Ben Webster — Bessie Smith — Bobby Hackett — Ethel Waters — Ben Pollack — James P. Johnson — Eubie Blake — Fats Waller — Vic Dickenson — Hot Lips Page — Louis Belson — Buddy Rich — Dave Tough — Willie "The Lion" Smith — Dizzy Gillespie — Fletcher Henderson — Charlie Parker — Don Redmond — Jack Teagarden — Benny Goodman — Sid Cattlett — Pops Foster — Benny Carter — Lucky Roberts — Johnny Hodges — Bix Beiderbecke — Bob Haggart — Yank Lawson — Buddy DeFranco — Bob Wilber — Gus Johnson — Benny Morton — Ralph Sutton, etc. I could go on and on. I trust that the artists whose names I did not cite will understand.

Among the greats who did come from New Orleans are Louis Armstrong — King Oliver — Jelly Roll Morton — Sidney Bechet — Eddie Miller — Johnny Dodds — Baby Dodds, and others. There are many more, of course, but in my opinion these names have had the greatest influence on other players. I agree, jazz came from everywhere.

JAZZ ABROAD

THE PHILOSOPHER

In 1947, I took Joe Bushkin (the well known pianist) and Herb Ward (the bassist) down to Rio de Janeiro to play a small night club in the Copacabana Palace Hotel. After playing as a trio for a week, we decided to add a drummer. BiBi Miranda, the famous black drummer from Lisbon, Portugal, was highly recommended to us. We heard him play one number and hired him. We loved him. He didn't use drumsticks. He played everything with his hands. He spoke English with a Portuguese accent, sounding all his "w's' 'as "v's."

Most of our customers were of the wealthiest Brazilian families. They loved our music and constantly invited us to their apartments and homes (not to play, but as guests). Now, BiBi had never been in the social presence of the rich whites, and when I invited him to come to a party one night, he declined, saying he wasn't certain he would be treated well. I convinced him everything would be fine, so he came. Upon seeing this luxurious life for the first time as a guest, he said, "Look, Bud, these people don't swing — they got everything. Ve sving — ve got shit."

JAZZ LIFE IN CHILE

Mario was the pianist in the jazz group that I led in Santiago, Chile. He spoke only Italian, but he insisted upon speaking English to me. The other musicians spoke only Spanish, and I found I had an easier time understanding *them*. However, Mario was hilarious and I loved trying to understand what he was trying to say in English. The first time I talked to him, he said, "Oh, Senor, I was so exciting to meeting you." When I broke up laughing, he seemed to understand, and he broke up too. Each night he would say to me, "Oh, Senor, you wassa no looka like a musich. You wassa looka like a gent. If I wassa wrong, donja tella me."

48

Mario had a problem. He adored women — especially married women. His timing was very bad, and he was forever jumping out of bedroom windows to evade an unexpected husband. On many occasions he would show up to play the piano, wearing one shoe. Just before I arrived in Chile, Mario was involved in an affair with a married woman with a high social standing. She adored him and when her husband heard about the affair, he dragged Mario into court. She threatened to kill herself if her husband did not withdraw the charges. Her husband complied with her wishes. One day I asked Mario how it all ended and he said, "Oh, Senor, I wassa very luck. If her husbanda is Italian, I am dead, but he issa Chilean."

THE BISHOP IS CONVERTED

The year I lived in Chile I was offered a job to play at El Carrera Hotel in El Boite. I organized a quintette made up of Chilean musicians, who were surprisingly good. They had heard American Jazz *only* on records. One night in a room adjacent to El Boite, a party was being given for twelve Maryknoll priests who had been imprisoned in China. In the middle of our first set, a priest, holding a large glass of scotch-and-soda and cigar to match, walked up to me and asked,
"Are you the Bud Freeman who played with Benny Goodman at the Paramount Theatre in New York?"
"Yes, Father I am," I said.
"Well, I was dancin' in the aisle," he said. His name was Father Manning, a hard-boiled, street fighting priest out of Brooklyn, who did much to help the Chinese victims of a war that seemed never to end. He is the only man I've ever known to have absolutely no regard for himself. He worked in a mission called "Boy's Town" in Talca, a small village near Santiago. He was a rabid Jazz fan who owned several hundred recordings of the best musicians in Jazz. We became close friends and since he refused ever to have any money that he could call his own, I invited him to lunch and dinner many times.
After several months of listening to records and discussing many subjects, I dared to ask him how a man of his high intelligence could accept the idea of God. He

completely broke up laughing and replied, "I'm in love with people."

Father Manning's immediate superior was the bishop of the mission. One day the bishop asked us what all this cacophonous noise was about, and Father Manning broke in with, "Oh, Your Grace, you mustn't say that — Jazz is a very religious music that one day will sweep the world." The bishop thought about this for a moment and turned to me and asked, "Mr. Freeman, do you think that Father Manning is a little odd?"

About a week later as Father Manning was entering his quarters, he heard his record player and wondered who could have turned it on. There lay the bishop on his side, head in hand, digging Count Basie's record of the "One O'clock Jump." When Father Manning's furlough to the states came up, the bishop told him that he could *not* take the records with him — that if he did, he was not to return to Chile.

MEN WITHOUT WOMEN

It took about six months for word to get around the Aleutian Islands that I had a good band. Calls came into the island of Adak every day, asking for our services, for which we were well paid.. We played all of the officers' clubs on the Aleutian chain and every mess hall on 'Adak.

One day. I received a call from a Major K. He said that he was giving a supper party and dance for the officers of his company, and that he would like to hire the band. I accepted the offer and after the major said good-bye, I had a double-take of thought. "Dance? — why there isn't a woman within three thousand miles of this island. Oh well, anything can happen in the army," I thought. A few nights later we arrived at the officers' club to play and could not believe what we saw. There was a buffet set up on a table thirty-feet long, filled with delicacies we had not seen since civilian life. There were plates of pate de foie gras, salmon, tuna, smoked turkey, chicken, roast beef, stuffed olives and artichokes. Tables were set for two, with candles and fancy tablecloths (the major must have made the tablecloths) and a small space was highly polished, to be used as a dance floor. It was evident that the Major had been an interior decorator in civilian life; he also built a bandstand with lights that changed color every two or three seconds. The Blue Angel couldn't compete with this (The Blue Angel was a popular nite-club in New York City). Just before we played our first number the Major sent us a tray of drinks; liquor was not easy for the enlisted man to acquire (Bourbon cost seventy-five dollars a quart). As the liquor flowed, our pianist who hadn't had a drink in over a year, got stoned out of his mind and danced with a colonel who didn't seem to mind, and upon seeing this the other officers got up from their tables and danced with one another. We in the band broke up laughing at all of this and proceeded to get pretty drunk ourselves. I'm not certain but I think the officers ended up playing our instruments.

The next day the Major called me to say that the General had severely reprimanded him. I said that I was sorry our pianist had danced with the Colonel. "Oh, I didn't mind, but the General doesn't understand," he replied About four weeks later the Major hired us for another party. Just before we started to play he slipped a note into my hand that read: "By order of the General, enlisted men are *not* to dance with officers."

I should like to offer my plagiaristic apologies to Ernest Hemingway; I could think of no title as appropriate as this.

DASHIEL HAMMET

I have always admired the great detective story writer, Dashiel Hammet, but never did I dream that I'd meet him, and of all places, in the Aleutian Islands. Dashiel enlisted in the army just to get away from the civilian life that existed in the states. He could easily have been an officer but since he saw through the politics of the military system, he went in as a private. He became a buck sergeant and refused to go any higher. The island on which we were based was the largest of the Aleutians and was thought of as the cosmopolitan island of the chain.

Dashiel edited a newspaper which he named the "Adakian." The paper was one of the most interesting I've ever read. It had an excellent cartoonist by the name of Bernard Anastasia, who today is a top art director in Chicago. Its editorials were written by highly knowledgeable authorities on China, Japan and Russia. Now, since Hammet edited everything that was written for the paper, the editorials were highly informative. There were truths about our Allies that could never have been printed in the States since everything had to favor the American forces. One day the General of the Alaskan command came down to ask Dashiel if the paper couldn't give its readers more news of the American forces progress. Dashiel's brilliant reply to this request was, "I'm sorry General, but this paper has a policy never to publish any ads." I was the leader of a band that toured the chain and Dashiel often came along to hear the band and get stoned. One night at an officers' party he took over the checkroom and mixed all their hats and coats so thoroughly that it took half the night to sort them out. Every enlisted man on the island loved him.

HE WAS IMPERVIOUS TO HONOR

I have said many times that Jazz is not taken as a serious art form in the United States. Most people think of it (if they think about it at all) as a sort of music that anyone can play. In Europe and the Orient, Jazz is taken seriously and is considered to be an art form. About six years ago I went to Japan with an all-star Jazz group made up of Jimmy Rushing, Pee Wee Russell, Buck Clayton, Vic Dickenson, Dick Cary, Cliff Leemans, Jack Lesberg and Eddie Condon. Eddie is a big name in Japan and about five minutes after we landed at the Tokyo airport, a carpet was rolled from the terminal to the plane. A Japanese airline hostess walked in military fashion to the plane, stopped and stood at attention. Condon came down the portable stairs of the plane. He was staggering drunk; his hat was tipped over one of his ears and his uncombed hair fell down over his eyes. His shirt tail hung out of his trousers and one of his shoes was missing. The girl presented Eddie with a beautiful bouquet of roses; she seemed not to be aware of his condition (as though this were normal for an American). She did a perfect about-face and walked back to the terminal. Eddie staggered to the terminal, roses in arm, giving the appearance of having just come from an Irish wake! James Joyce would have loved it!

THE ENGLISH

For years on end we Americans have been saying that the English are a stuffy, unfeeling people. On the contrary, to me they are the warmest, most gracious people I've ever met. Of course, I'm not generalizing, I'm simply talking about the English people I've known. About ten years ago, Gerald Lascelles (The Queen's cousin) and Lord Montague held a Jazz festival in Manchester, England and Dizzy Gillespie, Buck Clayton and I were invited to appear as soloists. I was amazed to find that the English were the most enthusiastic Jazz fans of all, and that we were much better known in England than in our own country. In fact we were famous. One day Lord Montague asked me to take his wife Belinda to the races and, of course, I said that I'd be delighted. I've been a horse player all my life. In England horse racing seems to be more of a sport and has much more dignity than American racing. The people are much more civilized and don't knock you down to get in a bet. One of the delights is in watching the bookmakers make hand signals to one another. A man who had had too much to drink was arguing with a bookmaker about a bet. It seemed that the drunk had bet on a horse other than the one he had intended to bet. The horse that he intended to bet won the race and in insisting that he be paid, the man threatened the bookmaker. The bookmaker's reply was, "I'll have your neck first!"

Lady Montague owned a stable of horses and, of course, she loved racing. We had lost the first two races, but in the third race there was a big black horse named "Big Brother." I asked Belinda about the form of the horse and she replied, "I think he's rather slow of foot." I played him just on a hunch and he won by six lengths and paid 16 to 1. Belinda was amazed, and said, "If you knew so much, why didn't you tell me?" Incidentally, the next day there was an item in *The Times* about it that read, "American Jazz musician picks winner at 16 to 1."

For the week of the jazz festival I stayed at the Midland hotel, the most posh in Manchester. A bellboy about twelve years of age announced that he would look after me for the week. He was impeccably dressed in a uniform and cap. He resembled a student at an old English military school. As he was preparing my bath, I asked him to get me a bottle of men's cologne. He looked at me rather quizzically not quite understanding what I wanted. But he came back with a small bottle of spray cologne. I gave him a half crown and he said, "Oh Sir, that's too much." As he opened the door to leave, he looked back and said, "Oh Sir, I should be very careful with that cologne if I were you. It's French you know."

THE CIVILIZED BRITISH

On a recent flight to London, England, the captain of the plane, who sounded more like a member of Parliament than a flight officer, made his usual announcements and then suddenly the plane hit an "air pocket," shaking us up quite a bit for a moment, after which the captain announced, "Sorry about the turbulence, ladies and gentlemen — we haven't mastered the weather yet. Perhaps next year. Thank you."

THE ANGLOPHILE

I think that my love for the British (Irishmen, please take no offense) began when I was about 16 years of age. I went to see "MacBeth," my first play, and fell completely in love with the language. I dreamed about going to Great Britain, not knowing of course, that I should become a Jazz musician, and finally be invited to play there. About thirteen years ago I played my first concert in Manchester, England, and by this time word had got around that I truly loved Great Britain. After the concert a gigantic football player, who was quite drunk came back stage to see me. He picked me up, embraced me and said, "What's all this rot about your being an anglophile? You're *one* of *us.*"

LENNIE FELIX

My experience in playing with British musicians has always given me the feeling that they don't know how good they are. On many occasions when I tried to compliment them, they invariably answered that: "You Americans do it much better." The British Jazz musicians have been exposed to our music for a long time now. There is

no reason why they shouldn't play it as well. As a matter
of fact, better. One such musician is the fine pianist
Lennie Felix. He has been absolutely devoted to Jazz all
of his life. I've had the great pleasure of playing with
him many times. He ought to come to the states for a
tour. The Americans would be surprised, and, in fact
they'd love him.

"All the best, Lennie."

IT'S NEVER TOO LATE TO BE YOUNG

Robert Linnsen, author of the book *Zen In Everyday
Life*, writes that True youth is psychological, I have known
many young people to be actually dead inside, and I have
known many old people to be very alive and hopeful.
One very alive gentleman whom I chanced to meet at the
'Two Brewers' in London, is 96 years young. He has been
frequenting the pub for sixty-one years. The first time that
I had the pleasure to talk with him, he asked me about
New York City. Did it have good theatre? Were there
many museums? Were the people conscious of the arts?
Did democracy really work? Was the mayor doing anything to lessen police graft? I was amazed to hear all of
this coming out of this delightful old man. In addition to
this he stood very erect and had a very majestic walk,
bending only when he saw a friend to whom he nodded
very politely. After several visits to the pub, he and I
became good friends. One day I asked him to deliver a
message to Michael Stanley, a well known actor, who frequented the pub. I left London for two weeks to play
some concerts and on my first day back I stopped in the
pub. Standing at the bar was my old friend. Upon seeing
me, he waved and asked about my tour. Then he said,
"Oh, by the way, your actor friend hasn't been in lately.
I couldn't give him your message."

"NOT TO WORRY"

Whenever I go to London I stay at the "White House,"
my favorite hotel there. The valet is one of the most
pleasant men I've ever met. He usually calls to ask if my
clothes need pressing and if I'm in a hurry, he picks them
up and says, "Not to worry, you'll have them back in

plenty of time." I enjoy betting on the races, and I must say that I've been very lucky, especially in London. One day he asked me what I liked in the last race. I selected a long shot and suggested that he put a pound on it to win. He thought about it for a moment and then asked, "Do you really think it will win, Sir?" The only answer that I could give him was, "Not to worry." The horse won at eighteen to one.

LONDON AIRPORT
On our recent tour of Great Britain we were met at the airport by our dear friend Nicol Williamson, the great actor. Nicol suggested that we go to a pub to make some plans for the day. The plans never left the pub.

ENGLISH HAS MANY TONGUES
There's an ancient language that's spoken in Yorkshire, England. A man and woman, who were very drunk, were quarreling in the street about 3 o'clock in the morning. They yelled at each other so loudly that I was awakened. I went to the window to see and to hear what it was all about, and this is what I heard the woman scream, "You're nothing but a thieving, fooking busted; You're a knave!!!!"

THE NOISY AMERICANS
I took a taxi from my hotel to Lennie Felix's apartment, and on the way over the driver asked,
"Are you from London, Sir?"
"No, I'm from New York," I said.
"Oh, I shouldn't have thought so," he said.
"Why do you say that," I asked.
"You're so quiet," he said.

PUB LIFE
There's a pub in London called the 'Two Brewers.' It's a sort of hangout for actors, writers, artists and musicians. I've never heard a dull word spoken there. One night an actress who was appearing in John Osborne's play, "West of Suez," introduced herself to me. "Mr. Freeman, I un-

derstand that you're an anglophile. I've never met one before."

Incidentally, Ralph Richardson was starring in the play. In my opinion he's the finest actor around.

NEVER WORRY ABOUT BEING LATE

In Great Britain people don't take appointments very seriously. I have many friends in London. I made an appointment one day with an old friend for lunch. I was an hour late and thought naturally that he had waited and then left. The next day I called him to apologize and he said, "Good heavens, did we have an appointment?"

THE BRAGGART

About six years ago I played a concert at the American Embassy in London. The hall held about 800 people and it was sold out. I, of course, was very happy with the response of the audience and left the next day thinking only of the good time I had. Just recently I met a reporter for the *London Observer* who told me that he attended the concert and this is what he wrote:

"Bud Freeman played a concert at the American Embassy last night and just about caused a riot. The hall holds only 800 people and more than two thousand showed up. They had to call out the Guard to quell what appeared to them to be a potential insurrection. Several people wrote to the newspapers complaining that although they bought tickets way ahead of the date of the concert, they were not allowed anywhere near the place."

My agent has *never* to this day mentioned this to me. I suppose he thought I'd ask for too much money to play a return date.

RELATIVITY

English lady to behemoth husband: "Do sit down dear. The room seems so small with you standing there."

DRUGSTORE IN LONDON

In the drugstore of the "White House" in London one day, as I waited for my change, a man standing next to me was biting open a small package. The girl who was waiting on him pleaded, "Please sir, don't do that with your teeth." The man without any attempt to be funny said, "Oh, they're not mine."

BACKSTAGE IN EDINBURGH

An elderly Scot came back stage to see me during the intermission of a concert I was playing. He had had quite a bit to drink and sort of stumbled into my dressing room. I quickly gave him a chair and as soon as he sat down, he took a flask out of his pocket and offered me a drink. I declined, explaining that I'd rather have a drink after the concert. He then took a big drink, turned to me and said, "Mr. Fraiman, I've been listening to your records since I was a boy." He later told me that he was 83 years old.

SUPPER IN EDINBURGH

Bank Hickok, who finances our band, invited us to supper at the George Hotel. The service was excellent but hurried because we had to play a concert and the maitre d' was putting pressure on the busboy to clear dishes away as soon as he saw an empty dish. Bob Haggart, who has a wonderful sense of the ridiculous and refuses to take himself seriously, was sitting impeccably dressed, when suddenly the hurried bus-boy dropped a dish of bearnaise sauce on his back. Bob, without taking any offense, asked, "May I have some mustard for my tie?"

BILLY NEEDS A DRINK

Billy Butterfield and I were walking into the waiting room at the Prestwick Airport in Scotland, when suddenly he spotted a bar. He had had a few too many and was told that the bars were closed. Upon seeing this open bar, he pulled me toward it and with great excitement said, "Look Bud, a bar. What a civilized country!"

JENNIFER FREEMAN GALLACHER

Ken Gallacher, the well known Scottish sports writer and Jazz critic, has bestowed upon me an honor I had never dreamed of having. About four years ago his wife had a child, a girl. During the period of her pregnancy I was touring Scotland and had the good fortune to meet her. I remember saying that I never had a child and that I doubted very much that I'd get married again. She smiled and promised that she'd name her child after me. Her name is Jennifer Freeman Gallacher. In twelve years we have a date for dinner. It's amazing what one can do with a saxophone!

FOREIGN RELATIONS

Everywhere in the world that Jazz musicians have played they've made thousands of friends. Everywhere in the world that diplomats have gone they've made enemies.

PARIS

In 1929 I went to Paris to see my friend Dave Tough. He was playing in a nightclub and restaurant called "L'Abbey" in Place Pigalle. It seemed to me to be the most cosmopolitan restaurant of its time. The Prince of Wales, later to become the King of England, used to sit in with the band on drums. F. Scott Fitzgerald frequented the place and he and Dave wrote limericks together. FuJita, the famous Japanese artist, was there with bangs and earrings doing the "Charleston." I remember asking Dave what he thought of the Prince of Wales' drumming and he said, "He might make a good king."

F. Scott Fitzgerald was fascinated with Dave's brilliant mind, and on many occasions he invited Dave to meet his literary friends, but Dave always declined. I think that he over-idolized many of the artists of his time. I had not seen him in a few years and upon seeing him in Paris for the first time, he asked how I liked Ernest Hemingway (Hemingway had just written "The Sun Also Rises"). When I confessed that I had not read the book, he was shocked, and didn't speak to me for about ten minutes. How could I, his best friend, not have read Hemingway? Dave had begun to write just before he died; he'd have become a fine writer.

A FEW OF MY FAVORITE PLACES

DETROIT, MICHIGAN

I have lived around the world most of my life. I've had favorite cities such as London, England; — San Francisco, California; — Lisbon, Portugal; — Paris, France; and Sydney, Australia. After having lived in all these cities, I came to realize that a city is its people. Some of the most charming people I have met live in Detroit, Michigan. I came here a year ago to play at the Sheraton Cadillac Hotel with the World's Greatest Jazz Band.

I received a call from Kay Savage, the famous food editor. She invited me to dinner at her home. One of her charming guests was Nancy Kennedy, the Women's editor of the "Ford Times." Nancy and I became friends immediately, and at the end of the evening she suggested that I was a writer.

I thought no more of it, and said "goodnight" — not knowing that I would ever see her again. The next day a messenger delivered six flair pens, and six notebooks to my hotel, with a note suggesting that I start writing that day. I wrote a few anecdotes, and then called Nancy. We had lunch together. She read what I had written, and seemed to be very pleased with my writing. I was very flattered, because Nancy is considered to be one of the finest editors in the country. Now, after a year of writing, I have a book. In the time it has taken me to write this book, I have made many new friends.

Just recently I ran into Bob Chester, the famous band leader of the 40's. I had not seen him in over thirty years. Detroit is his home; he was born here. We reminisced about the early days in New York City. The endless nights in Harlem . . . listening to all our favorite jazz musicians. We remembered that the only addiction we had was the music itself, and then I casually asked him if he ever smoked marijuana. He said that he had "tried it a couple times," and decided that it wasn't good for him. I asked him why, and he replied, "One day after having smoked a whole stick of it, I found myself standing in front of my hotel without a stitch of clothes on!"

THE LELAND HOUSE

Never, in all my travels have I seen a hotel quite like The Leland House in Detroit, Michigan. To begin, it has a twenty-four hour police guard made up of young, educated, swinging, well-dressed, well-mannered men. The girls who take care of the desk and phone are lovely, well educated and charming. There's a coffee shop called 'Biff's' in the building that makes the best tuna sandwich I've ever tasted. All the apartments have refrigerators and cooking facilities. There's a store in the building that sells anything your appetite desires. On the fourth floor there's a bar, lounge and recreation room, including a sauna bath. The people who reside at the hotel are the friendliest and most courteous people one would want to meet. I truly believe that if a thief broke into The Leland House he'd end up living there, saying to himself, "At last I've found a safe place to live."

Rubinoff, the famous violinist, who's about eighty years old, lives there. He has a suite made up of mementos and memorabilia that allow one *no* place to sit or lie down. There's an old, well known anecdote about him that's worth repeating. During his popular days at N.B.C., he demanded more respect there than *anyone* in radio. One day the great "Heifitz," entered the artists' elevator and was told that he'd have to take the employees elevator. Heifitz, of course, said, "But, I'm Heifetz, the violinist." The man running the elevator growled back, "I don't give a damn if you're Rubinoff, you can't use this elevator."

Jack Brake, the manager of the Leland House, differs from other hotel managers in that he actually loves people. Many well-known show people and musicians stay at his hotel because of his charm. His love for people starts at home; he has nine children. I've tried to invite him out to dinner many times, but he always insists that we dine in his apartment. His fourteen-year-old son cooked for us one night. He's really good. Jack will never be lonely. His children love him.

THE INTELLECTUAL CLOTHING SALESMAN

There is a clothing salesman who works in Richman Brothers in Detroit, Michigan. His name is Bill Fulmer and he is one of humanity's closest friends. I knew him a year before I knew he was a good drummer. In fact, he has a better beat than some drummers who are well known. Bill is one of the best-read men I have ever known. If one were to drop in on him every day, Bill could be found sitting next to a rack of clothes reading a book or some esoteric magazine.

People from all over the country drop in to visit him: famous athletes, actors, writers, composers, and horn players, who buy all their clothes from him. Bill never tries to sell anything to anybody. He lets people sell themselves and as a result, his income allows him enough money to live the good life. He is very involved with people, constantly coming to their aid. When I asked how a man of his high intellect could work in a clothing store, he smiled and said that his job brought him close to all the walks of life and without that, he couldn't be happy.

One day, I picked out a suit, tried it on and asked Bill what he thought. "I don't like it; why don't you wait until we get something good," he said. Since then, I haven't looked into a clothing store other than this one.

Bill plays concerts and club dates in the Detroit area and I think that he has more fun than any of us in the full-time professional ranks.

THE GIRL WITH THE GRANDFATHER COMPLEX

I have been playing golf for 35 years. The other day, I met an old friend on the Belle Isle Golf Course in Detroit, Michigan. I had not seen him in many years. His name is Dave Wilborn, former guitarist with McKinney's Cotton Pickers, the great band of the twenties and the thirties. Dave is retired, but plays occasionally at jam sessions. He told me that he was divorced and having the time of his life.

"You know, Bud, I'm 67 years of age and going with a girl 19," he said.

"How wonderful, you must be very happy," I said.

"Well, Bud, I'll tell you. She's great, but everytime

I see her, she says, 'Grandfather will you buy me a mink coat?' "

A NIGHT OFF

The 'Villanova' was one of the best Italian restaurants in New York City. It was the favorite of many musicians and actors. During a tour of one-nighters with Tommy Dorsey, Tommy invited me to have dinner there. He loved Italian cuisine. As we entered the restaurant, Tommy recognized a musician who had passed out in his chair, his head resting on the table. Tommy pointed to his friend and said, "Do you see that guy? He's one of the best flute players in the world, but not tonight."

SAN FRANCISCO

Although London, England is my favorite city, I could be talked into living in San Francisco, California; it maintains a great deal of charm in spite of the new buildings. The air is clear, and the sun shines more often there than it shines in parts of California that are *supposed* to be sunny. We — The World's Greatest Jazz Band — played a two-day engagement in San Francisco recently. The place that we played is called "Earthquake McGoons" — a nightclub in an old hotel that appears as something out of the Klondike, Gold Rush days. Clancy Hayes, the famous singer-banjo player, is unable to work because of his illness — I think he has cancer. We were asked to play a benefit for him. We played five sell-out shows in two days. There's a great deal of interest in Jazz music in San Francisco; the people seem to be hungry for it. There's also a turnover of creative thought; a thing that I have found to be missing in other large cities. It reminds me of Chicago in the twenties; the art colony on Rush Street; the many clubs that featured Jazz; and the constant talk, not of money, but of creative ideas.

JAZZ AND ALL THAT VAIL

Is there a ski resort in the world more beautiful than Vail, Colorado? We played there recently at a place called "Out Back," a restaurant-niteclub. The Club was packed every night; the people are starved for Jazz. Two

65

of the most rabid Jazz fans I've ever known are Larry and Marge Burdick, who own the "Red Lion Inn," the best restaurant in Vail. They differ from most restauranteurs in that they're more interested in people than the restaurant business; and yet their place is the most elegant there. Of course, they're people of excellent manners and taste. Larry Burdick's love for Jazz started when he was about eight years old. He was taking piano lessons from an old-fashioned music teacher. The teacher used to rap Larry's knuckles if his fingers were not placed exactly the way the teacher wanted them to be placed. Now Larry spent most of his practicing time listening to Louis Armstrong records, and one day during a lesson he suggested to his teacher, "How about putting a little Jazz feeling into these exercises?"

The teacher nearly had a stroke and that was about the end of Larry's piano lessons. I am reminded of my early music lessons. What pompous asses the teachers of that time were! They always gave me the impression that they thought they were doing me a favor.

The Burdicks have done more for Jazz in Vail than anybody. I hope they never leave.

SOME FAVORITE PEOPLE

CLEVELAND AMORY

Our band was enjoying a much needed holiday and during this time, I stopped off in Detroit to visit Nancy Kennedy, the editor of this book. I was invited to appear on the J. P. McCarthy show, a very popular lunch-hour radio interview. Just before my time to be interviewed, I was delighted to meet Cleveland Amory who was on the show. I had just read his excellent review of Cass Canfield's new book, and I mentioned how much I enjoyed the review. Cleveland Amory is a brilliant, gracious, witty, outspoken man! He thanked me and said, "How does one review a publisher?" I had never seen Mr. Amory before this meeting; I had thought of him as being a social register playboy who could write and say what he pleased because he could afford to. How wrong could I have been? He is a man completely devoted to curing all of life's sickness. Although he is very serious about every issue he speaks, he can't resist being funny about it, because he would prefer not to have his listener think that *he* thinks he's God. He quoted Somerset Maugham: "We like to see our friends get ahead, but not too far."

He talked about Don Rickles on the Hugh Hefner Playboy television show. Don was asking for Hugh Hefner: "Where's that dummy with the pipe?" There were endless gems of wit flowing from Mr. Amory. The funniest I thought was about Hugh Hefner's T.V. personality: "It's midway between technical difficulty and a station break."

As Mr. Amory was leaving, a little old lady tugged on my sleeve and said, "Mr. Freeman, will you tell Mr. Amory that I have a sister in Cleveland"?

BUDDY EBSEN

Buddy Ebsen, the star of the popular T.V. series "The Beverly Hillbillies" and the current "Barnaby Jones," was a famous dancer as far back as the 30's. He has always loved music, and to this day he goes out of his way to

hear a good band. Again, in 1937, I was playing with
Tommy Dorsey at the Commodore Hotel in New York
City. Buddy was appearing on Broadway, and he used to
come to hear the band about three times a week. One
night, in an inspired mood, he went into one of his dance
routines. An elderly woman dancing next to him reached
for his hand to shake it. "Young man you're a wonderful
dancer. You oughta be on the stage!!!," she raved.

RECORD SESSION

Bill Fulmer and his wife Lenore invited me to a party
at their home. Dave Wilborn and Tommy Saunders of the
"New McKinney's Cotton Pickers" were there.

The Fulmers are rabid jazz fans. They have a fine collection of records. As the liquor flowed and the music
inspired enthusiastic words about what was being played,
a repetition of the phrase "that's a bitch" was heard every
minute over a period of four hours. Through all of this
cacophony, Lenore Fulmer sat in the background, not
uttering a sound. She is a very polite, and gracious person. In a sober moment, I looked at Lenore, concerned
of course about what she was thinking. "How do you like
it," I asked. "It's a bitch," she replied.

LARRY CARTER

Larry Carter is a feature writer for the *Detroit News*.
He's one of the finest men I have ever been privileged
to know.

One day he called me to ask for an interview. I had
the feeling I had known him all my life. We talked about
the early jazz days in Chicago. It would appear that we
have hundreds of mutual friends. We could talk for days
on end about the wonderful musicians and show people
we knew in the 20's and 30's. To mention a few — Louis
Armstrong, Lucky Roberts, Buck and Bubbles, Jellyroll
Morton, Clarence Williams, Ethel Waters, Bessie Smith,
Fletcher Henderson and Eubie Blake. There's no end to
the names. Our delightful talks resulted in Larry's writing
an article about me in the *Detroit News*. He wrote a
beautiful paragraph about my instrument, the tenor saxophone. I asked his permission to quote him.

"The tenor saxophone is a male instrument. This is no mere

male chauvinist opinion. It is simply a fact. Like the cello, trombone, bassoon, and baritone horn, it makes deep, glorious, musical sounds. In the language of music, the sounds seem to denote masculine gender. In the hands of a master, the tenor can be subtle, boisterous, demanding yet coy, and often pleading in manner."

Would that I could live up to that!

THE MAN IN THE GREY TORN SWEATER

About six years ago, Yank Lawson, the trumpet player, was playing at Eddie Condon's. One night a drunk in a grey torn sweater stepped up to the bandstand and put his hand out as if in a gesture to shake hands with Yank. Yank shook the drunk's hand and found what he thought to be a dollar bill in it. The drunk mumbled something that Yank couldn't understand and returned to his table. Yank threw the bill on the piano and thought no more of it. The drunk repeated this gesture twice more and Yank casually threw the money on the piano. At the end of the set Yank watched the manager put the drunk out. Yank picked up the tip money to give each man in the band his share and instead of finding three one-dollar bills, he found three one-hundred dollar bills!

TENNIS ANYONE?

In 1937 Don Budge and Gene Mako were considered to be the best tennis players in the world. They had a problem; they loved to play the drums. Dave Tough and I were playing at the Commodore Hotel in New York City with Tommy Dorsey and his orchestra. Don and Gene used to take turns sitting in with the band. We wondered why such great athletes would want to bang on the drums; we didn't realize that they were serious about it. They were constantly asking Dave Tough questions about technique such as how and when to use the foot pedal, when to use the cymbals, when to use the snare drum, and when to play softly. Now Dave Tough was the last person ever to accept the idea that talent could be imparted to anyone who didn't have it. He answered all their questions as politely as he could, telling himself that one day he would ask them some questions about tennis. His day was to come sooner than he realized. Don and Gene in-

70

vited Dave and me to Forest Hills one day to watch them play. With all due respect to these fine tennis players, Dave and I were not especially interested in tennis. On the way back to the city, after the match, Gene Mako asked Dave how he liked the game. Dave couldn't wait to answer, "Oh it's very interesting, but when someone hits the ball at you why don't you duck?" Don and Gene gave up the drums shortly after that.

THE ART CRITIC

Mischa Resnikoff, the painter, was one of the first artists to work in the style of painting that Jackson Pollack was to make famous. The technique of this style was to tip a bucket of mixed paint, letting it drip onto a canvas.

Mischa loved musicians and invited many of them to his home in New York. Zutty Singleton, the famous drummer, had come to New York from California to stay with Mischa for a month. One day I went to visit Mischa and to see this new style of painting. I asked Zutty what he thought of Mischa's painting and he replied, "Man, that cat paints paint!"

TIME TO BRAG AGAIN

In the late thirties there was a Jazz critic who idolized Lester Young, the great tenor sax player. He idolized Lester more than any other critic had ever idolized a musician. He particularly disliked my playing and refused to own any of my recordings. Just recently I met the critic at a party and this is what he volunteered to tell me: "Bud, I owe you an apology and a compliment. Twenty years ago I had the honor to entertain Lester Young at my home. After dinner we went into my den to play some records. I was so pleased to be entertaining my idol. I asked him what recordings I could play for him. His immediate request was, 'You got any Bud Freeman?' "

A GUY NAMED JOE

In the early thirties, I free-lanced a great deal with the Dorsey Brothers, Bix, Benny Goodman, Joe Venuti, Eddie Lang, Fats Waller, Gene Krupa and the Great Louis Armstrong. We played many week-end parties at colleges and prep schools — especially Princeton which was a Jazz-oriented school. Everytime we played at Princeton, some guy by the name of Joe would sit in on piano. Since we weren't especially impressed with his playing, we never took the trouble to know his full name. But, there he was every time.

I was not to see him again until 1948. I was playing at the Blue Note in Chicago with one of those Condon-put-together bands. The men in the group were: Eddie Condon (now and then on guitar), Zutty Singleton on drums, Bobby Hacket on trumpet, Peanuts Hucko on clarinet, Dave Bowman on piano, Chuck Peterson on bass and myself on tenor. We played five nights a week, taking Sundays and Mondays off (incidentally, this was the only decent thing the Musicians' Union had ever done for its musicians).

My brother, the actor, was appearing in Tennessee Williams' play, "A Streetcar Named Desire." He called me to say that José Ferrer, the great actor, was in town; that he, José, loved jazz and wanted to meet me. I was very pleased because José Ferrer was my favorite actor at that time. My brother brought him down to the Blue Note. I didn't see them come in and when I finished the set, my brother came to the bandstand and took me to his table to meet the great actor. Upon meeting him, I stepped back as though in a state of shock and howled, "For God's sake, Joe — are you José Ferrer????!!!!"

THE SWINGING JUDGE

The most unique Judge ever to enter the world of jurisprudence, in my opinion, is Peter B. Spivak, Judge of Common Pleas Court, in Detroit, Michigan. I had the pleasure to lunch with him recently at the Detroit Athletic Club. He's a tall, long-haired, boot-footed, mod dresser who resembles a young Dave Garroway. He's brilliant, gracious, modest, gregarious, and kind. I was very surprised to find that he's a rabid Jazz fan and is aware of all the important soloists in Jazz.

He told me that he was criticized for wearing long hair. I wish I had been there to defend him; I'd have reminded his critics that moss doesn't grow on the "Rolling Stones." But Judge Spivak needed no defense; he probably knows more about law than all of his contemporaries put together. The long hair stayed. If Judge Peter B. Spivak is an example of what the Supreme Court Judges are to be, we're going to have the fairest law this country has ever known.

MARTHA RAYE

About a month before the Roger Wolfe Kahn band broke up, we worked at the Sun and Surf Club on Long Island. The band played a floor show that featured The Ritz Bros., Nick Long and Eunice Healy (a fine dance team), and on weekends an unknown comedian by the name of Milton Berle, who did a comedy routine and acted as Master of Ceremonies. Our vocalist was a quiet, almost shy girl by the name of Martha Raye. Martha was a fine singer; she was more interested in singing ballads than anything else. I used to see her sitting on the beach by herself, reading or singing softly some new song. I did not know that she was gregarious, until one night after the last show she knocked everybody out by doing a perfect imitation of the Ritz Bros.' routine. She had studied their act from the bandstand and learned it in a week. Now the Sun and Surf Club was a hangout for all the top theatrical agents in New York and I'm certain that this impromptu skit launched Martha Raye into becoming a comedienne. Long after she became a star, she came to a place I played in Connecticut one night and sang with my group all night.

I have often wondered if she really wanted to be a comedienne. She really loved to sing!

DAVE GARROWAY

The first time that I heard of Dave Garroway, he had a radio show in Chicago. I was especially fascinated by his sincere interest in Jazz music, his actual study of the background of each artist he talked about. He particularly liked Sidney Bechet, and talked about Bechet in a beautiful poetic way, enabling the listener to feel what the artist was trying to say. Although Bechet was well on his way to becoming a commercial success, there can be no doubt that Garroway's devotion helped a great deal. Dave's popularity grew so tremendously that at one time I had the

73

feeling that he owned Chicago (in an artistic sense, that is). I could never understand why he gave all of this up to go to New York.

The entertainment that went into the Blue Note, the well-known Chicago Jazz Club, was handled by Dave, and *never* did anything appear there that wasn't of the best taste in Jazz. I'm certain that he did more to create Jazz interest in Chicago than anyone since the Louis Armstrong days. I talked to him just before he went to New York and I had a feeling that he was ambivalent about leaving Chicago. But he left to take over a news and weather television show that went on the air at seven o'clock in the morning. How he was able to do this all those years, I'll never know; it meant getting up at four o'clock every morning. I appeared on the show several times and always had to stay up all night to make the rehearsal, which started at five. Dave was the only man alive who could make a bad weather report sound interesting. His listeners were always charmed by his words. I doubt very much that they ever remembered what the weather was to be on that given day. The show became, of course, the most popular of its time; there was not an important person in show business who didn't try to appear on it. Unlike other television personalities, Dave Garroway never seemed career bound. He seemed rather to be interested in people, especially creative people, and in the injustice that existed in the world. It is a pity that we don't see more of him on television. He's a dedicated man.

THE GREAT BING

Millions of words have been written on how to succeed in business or in whatever profession one might choose to follow. But one of the few truly successful men in history ever to dispel these theories is Bing Crosby. I have known him since 1929 and he did it all having a ball. Many entertainers, singers, band leaders and what not have stepped over people to make it. Not Bing; he stepped under them. To begin, he truly loved music. He idolized people like Bix and Louie and to this day he loves and admires people with talent. Just recently he invited our band, The World's Greatest Jazz Band, to play his annual Pebble Beach party for the finest golfers in the world. When he greets you, he looks at you as though you were the only person there. I have never seen him do an unkind thing. I doubt very much that he has ever given any thought to self-importance. I'll never forget the time that I first recorded with him. I was not feeling too well, but didn't want to say so. About half way through the session he came over to me and asked if I was feeling all right. Then he felt my forehead and said, "Bud has a fever, let's break it up." And that was the end of the session. On another recording date with an orchestra of thirty-two men, things weren't going the way he liked, so he reached into his back pocket and pulled out thirty-three tickets to the ball game. "Let's not waste this beautiful day trying to do something that isn't going to come off." With all of his wealth he still wants to work and search for new ideas. He'll never grow old.

THE HUNT CLUB

In 1940 "The Summa Cum Laude" got a job in a joint called the Hunt Club. The Club was on 47th Street between 6th and 7th Avenues in New York City. The block was made up of small hotels, stores and bars which were the hangouts of pimps, whores, dope peddlers, thieves and gunmen. The police gave them no trouble; of course, there were the usual payoffs. The Hunt Club was owned and operated by one Danny Morse, an underworld character. Danny had a bad limp in his right leg, giving him the appearance of one carrying a ball and chain. It seemed not unlikely that he could at one time have worn a ball and chain; he had been in *so* many prisons. But he was as *gentle* as he was *tough*. In fact, he was an excellent well-mannered host. Our band attracted an elegant class of people (Jazz music has always fascinated them) and the place became the rendezvous of every celebrity in town. When Danny saw these people he moved all the underworld characters into the front bar and put up a velvet curtain to separate the bar from the night club. He then hired a doorman, an ex-pickpocket, who politely helped people in and out of taxis and private limousines. The boss reminded him every night that he was not to pick any pockets. The doorman's retort was always the same: "Aw boss, it'd be too easy — I wouldn't get no kicks out of it."

One night, John O'Hara, the famous novelist, got into

a fight in the bar! John was drinking heavily in those days and could be nasty. The boss came into the bar yelling, "Don't lay a hand on this man; he's different than us."

Alexander King, the humorist, and Frank Norris, the novelist, asked me to introduce them to a safe-cracker one night. They talked for a few minutes and, after shaking hands with the safe-cracker, Alex and Frank went back to their table. I asked the safe-cracker if he knew the men he had just talked to and he replied, "Who'd know anybody like that? We never meet the people we rob. We'd be embarrassed to meet them on a social level."

We played at the Hunt Club for six months and went directly from there to the Sherman Hotel in Chicago. Jazz music is the only kind of music that can travel from rags to riches to rags in one season.

KNOWLES ROBINS

One of the wildest, most brilliant men I have ever met was a student at the University of Chicago by the name of Knowles Robins. His family had written a French textbook that was widely used in schools throughout the country. Knowles was very interested in jazz music and loved to hang out with us whenever we went to hear our favorite musicians. One morning about seven o'clock, after having been out all night listening to Louis Armstrong, Knowles invited us to sleep at his fraternity house at the university. The man who had played the carillon for years on end suddenly became ill and called Knowles to ask him to substitute for him. Knowles obliged by playing "Yes, We Have No Bananas" on the carillon. He was expelled for this and returned two years later to become the best French professor the university ever had. When he later went to Paris for the first time, to lecture in French, he was asked where he got such a beautiful accent and he replied, "In Chicago."

HOAGY'S WEDDING

Sometime in the thirties, Hoagy Carmichael got married — I think it was the first time for him. He called me and asked me to round up some jazz buddies for a jam session at his apartment. I called Bunny Berigan, Joe Bushkin, Dave Tough, and Pee Wee Russell. We had a ball; it was one of the best Jazz groups I've ever heard. George Gershwin was there listening to every note the group played. I've always thought of him as a creative artist, but he was an unsmiling sort of man who appeared to me to be rather ego-maniacal. I'll never forget the expression on his face when I played about ten improvised choruses of his classic "I've Got Rhythm." He seemed actually to be in pain. He died shortly after that.

JOSEPH SYRON: BON VIVANT, RACONTEUR, DENTIST!

Joseph Syron is a dentist in the Fisher Building in Detroit, Michigan. He's a swinging playboy and the best dentist in town. I had the good fortune to meet him about two years ago. In that short period, he has cleaned my teeth ten times. Actually, I have never made an appointment with him. I simply call when I get into town to say, "hello," and he says, "Hi Buzz, come on over." I asked him one day what made him become a dentist and he said, "Oh, I guess I just wanted to *see* what people had to say."

If, since the inception of dentistry, there had been a few thousand Joe Syrons in the world, I doubt very much that people would ever have had to wear false teeth.

THE CONVICTS LOST A FRIEND

Paul Fink, ex-policeman, ex-warden's assistant, ex-owner of the Padded Cell (a jazz club in Minneapolis) is the dearest friend a convict or any other man ever had. When he worked as an assistant to the warden of a well-known prison, the convicts loved him so much that they used to tell him the day before a planned prison break: "Paul, we're gonna have a break tomorrow; stay in your office — we don't want you to get shot." I had the great pleasure to work for Paul at his jazz club. He loved music more than business and when a customer talked too loudly, Paul would ask him politely to soften his conversation or leave. Paul is a big, round, giant of a man who can really handle himself in a fight but he prefers to love people. At present, he is the owner of a bar and grill in the Wall Street Section of San Francisco. The place is simply called

'Paul Fink's.' It is an elegant little bar that caters to wealthy businessmen who love Paul. He is thinking about opening another jazz club. What happy news for the jazz world if he does! Incidentally, on the day he quit his job as assistant warden, the prisoners went on strike.

SOCIOLOGY AND ALL THAT JAZZ!

LOVE WILL FIND A WAY

Many years ago when things were a little different than they are today, John Bubbles, the great black dancer, was having an affair with a New York socialite, and in order to get into the posh building where she lived, he wore a janitor's outfit.

OBSERVATION

For years on end the whites have been brain-washed into believing that on every street corner in the south, one could see "darkies" laughing. The "darkies" aren't laughing anymore.

HAIR

About five years ago I played a tour of jazz concerts all through Europe with the Newport Jazz Festival All Stars. As our bus pulled into Helsinki, Finland, Coleman Hawkins, the great tenor man, was quite drunk, and having a serious argument with another black musician. It seems that this musician had said something unkind to Hawkins and Hawkins responded with,

"Man, where did you get that beauty parlor hairdo?"

The man shot back with "I wish you wouldn't talk like that in front of all these blue eyes" ('Blue eyes' is a term used by black musicians sometimes in talking about the whites). Hawkins tore open his shirt and screamed,

"Look at my hair. My mother had good hair, my father had good hair, and I got good hair. And what's more, Bud Freeman's blacker than you are."

THE JAZZ BANDIT

Tommy Felony had come of a long line of safe-crackers and thieves. When he reached the age of six, his parents were shocked to see that he took no interest in playing with his toy acetylene torch, but rather preferred to bang away on an old stolen piano that stood in a corner of their hiding-room.

"I'll never understand these modern day children — when I was his age, I had my fingers in everybody's pockets," said his mother.

His father suggested they steal a saxophone for the boy but his mother objected, saying that it would be better to wait until their boy was old enough to do his own stealing. Why deprive him of the pleasures they had had when they were young?

"I guess you're right," said his father. — "And what's more, there's his private tutoring in safe-cracking and nitro-glycerine tests to come. Incidentally, I saw a quack the other day who told me that we should have Tommy's fingertips filed now, so that he won't have to go through the painful ordeal of having it done when he's older."

After the boy's fingertips were filed, he ceased to bang on the piano. Instead, he began smashing things with an old crow-bar his father had left about. Upon hearing this noise, his father reasoned that he had better do something in a hurry to deter the boy from banging, if the boy was to have any kind of hopeful future as a safe-cracker. Obviously, there were years of mouse-quiet discipline to practice before one cracked his first safe. The only thing to do for the present was to get the saxophone and hope, of course, that the boy would tire of it, and get back to his natural interests. But this was not to be: the boy began to play (without any lessons) such songs as "Oh, Say Can You See the Combination of this Safe" and parts of the piano theme music from the "Great Train Robbery." Of course, his parents were terribly distressed with all this! Where had they erred? What had gone wrong with their geneology? Oh yes, the mother remembered having heard of a grandfather who opened a lock with a baton. Could this have something to do with the boy's strange behavior?

As time passed, the boy did become something of a jazz musician. He could play, "The Jazz Me Blues," "Muscat Ramble," and "Doodle-Dee-Doo." This, obviously, was sufficient to get him a job in almost any jazz-band.

His parents, with a great deal of reluctance, gave up on him as being a lost cause. One day, the boy saw his father weeping and asked what was the matter. His father looked at him sadly and said, "Tom, the most tragic thing to befall a man is that he outlive his talent. Thank the devil, this can never happen to you."

That night, the boy out of a sense of guilt, broke into a jewelry store and stole a diamond necklace valued at several thousand dollars. He was nabbed, arraigned, convicted and sent to jail for five years. His parents were appreciative of his effort, but thought what a wasted life, to have spent all those years playing jazz music, when he could have become a first-rate safe-cracker.

"They oughta pass a law making jazz music a misdemeanor," said his father.

NOT MANY OLD WRITERS AROUND

I've just finished reading Budd Schulberg's fine book, *The Four Seasons of Success*.

I have been around writers all of my life, and have found them to be (to say nothing of myself) the most troubled people I've ever known. Although Budd Schulberg has given many valid reasons for their being the way they are, I still wonder why most of them have never cared to live very long.

Every time a famous writer (who appeared to be at the peak of his career) committed suicide, my friend, the very humorous Dave Tough, would say, "Oh well, I suppose he couldn't have any more fun."

If I were to compare writers with musicians, I could say that I see a lot of old, out-of-work musicians around, but I don't see any old, out-of-work writers around. Is it possible that musicians may know something about life that writers don't know, that art may not be as important as life itself?

THE BROKEN CONTRACT

There are two kinds of musicians: those who love music and those whose only interest lies in making money. One of the latter was a banjo player who worked at NBC for twenty-three years. When, finally, he was fired, his only reaction was, "A contract doesn't mean a thing. They told me this was going to be a steady job."

THE MONEY GAME

A jazz musician who was sponsored by a millionaire was

asked by a rabid fan how it felt to be subsidized. "Well, I'll tell you," said the musician, "when I was a kid, I lived in a very poor neighborhood. There was a rich kid in the neighborhood who had a new, expensive football. If we didn't play the game according to his rules, he picked up the football and went home."

PROVERB

"Early to bed, early to rise makes a man lethargic, miserable, and demise."

CLIFF ROBERTSON

Just recently Cliff Robertson, the actor-producer-director, appeared on the Dick Cavett show. Cliff is married to Dina Merrill, the actress. I was especially impressed with Cliff's human feeling for the cow puncher — the rodeo man — and the cowboy stunt man. His forthcoming movie is about the life and courage of one of these men. In telling about these people, Cliff spoke of American heritage and culture. He said, "Unless a man is a Jazz musician, he doesn't have any American culture that he can call his own." Now Dick Cavett allowed this remark about jazz music to get away without his paying the slightest bit of attention to it. Indeed, jazz music is the only true American art form! Everywhere I go I hear people mentioning names of jazz musicians — of their most vital contrbution to American culture. I wonder, is there a whole new cognizance of Jazz in this country? Wouldn't it be wonderful?

Thank you, Cliff Robertson!

JAZZ IS FOR EVERYBODY

In a time long before the Jazz critic, a musician was judged by other musicians. If a man could really play, he became famous through word of mouth. We're forever reading about how jazz can only be played by the black man and yet Dave Tough, the great white drummer, was considered by the black musicians to be the best of his time. Louis Armstrong told me that he used to listen to Bix (the great white cornet player) whenever he had the chance. A perfect example of what I mean to say has to do with the time the great Jack Teagarden, a white trombone player, was playing in a white band that alternated with Fletcher Henderson's band (the best black band of its time) at the famous Roseland Ballroom in New York City. After Teagarden's first set the whole Henderson band came over to him and yelled, "Boy what are you doin' up there. Come on over with us where you belong." There is no doubt in my mind that whites play and feel the music just the same as the blacks. I'm thinking (of course) only of the very talented whites. Come to think of it there are many blacks who have *no beat* in their playing at all.

A POINT OF VIEW

John O'Hara wrote: "F. Scott Fitzgerald thought that rich people were different than other people, and when he found that they weren't, he was terribly disillusioned."

I have found many rich people to be lethargic and dull and I have found many to be creative and happy. I have nothing against money; it's just that I've never been able to do what one has to do to get a lot of it. I have had a full rich life — in fact, so luxurious that anyone who inherits what I have will be in debt. I do not believe that one has to keep busy to be happy. Loafing can be an art. Of course, one can loaf better with money. If I had it all to do over again, I don't think I'd change many things. I wish that I could afford to live the way I live.

MUSIC HATH CHARM

Henry Peacham, the seventeenth century British essayist, who wrote of chamber music said, "I dare affirm there is no science in the world that so affecteth the free and generous spirit with a more delightful and inoffensive recreation or better disposeth the mind to what is commendable and virtuous."

Henry, it's a pity that you didn't know Jazz.

THE EDUCATED

One day I visited a young professor, a Jazz fan, at Oxford University. As we sat having a sandwich and tea, his six-year-old daughter entered his chambers and introduced herself to me. I invited her to share some of my sandwich, but she declined, saying, "No thank you, sir I'm rather fastidious about such things."

THE ATHEIST

Today, our environment is flooded with books and movies of Dons and Godfathers. It all reminds me of a time in my youth when I played at an Italian wedding in Chicago. The bride-to-be was the daughter of a notorious Don.

The priest was late for the ceremony and the Don became very upset. He walked over to the bandstand and asked me to play some music until the priest arrived. He complained to me that religion was a big racket, and then he added, "You take-da the Pope, when he getsa seek, he senda for the besta doc in da world. He no wanta go to Heaven, he wanta stay right here. He gotta beega racket."

WHAT COLOR WOULD YOU LIKE US TO BE?

Vic Dickenson (the trombone player), Ruby Braff (the cornet player) and I were driving from New York City to Baltimore to play on a television show. As we reached the outskirts of Wilmington, Delaware, we spotted a diner just off the highway. Ruby suggested that we stop at the diner for some coffee and a snack. Vic said that he didn't think he'd be served there (this was about fifteen years ago) and we argued that they'd have to serve him so we went into the diner and sat down in a booth. Surely enough, the waitress called Ruby and me into the kitchen and asked,

"Is that fellow colored?"

"We all are," snapped Ruby. Before the waitress had a chance to say anything, we were all out the door. After our rehearsal for the television show, we were wined and dined by the producer in a very elegant restaurant.

RACIAL PREJUDICE

It's unfortunate that most people don't know as much about life as musicians. Long before it dawned on the ignorant whites that black people were also human beings, the black and white musicians lived together, played their music together, and treated one another with kindness and respect. About four years ago, I played a concert tour in Europe with an all-black band and they treated me beautifully. In about 1937 I was playing with Tommy Dorsey and staying at the Forest Hotel, an old theatrical hotel in New York. The Cotton Club had moved downtown from Harlem and of course it had an all-black revue and Cab Calloway's band. The club was just down the block from my hotel and many of the musicians in Cab's band used to visit me. During one of the tours with Tommy Dorsey, I came down with a virus which laid me up for about ten days. Every day that I was ill the girls in the chorus and the musicians came to see me. The word on the street was, "Go on up and see Bud Freeman, he's very sick and they're having a ball."

During the Second World War I spent 22 months in the Aleutian Islands. I was stationed at Adak, where there were about ten thousands black troops. We lived together very peacefully without the slightest thought of race, until some idiot came along to make trouble. People can live together if they're given a chance.

THE FREEDOM OF PLAYING JAZZ

Unlike other musicians the Jazz musician has absolute freedom in his music. The musicians in the studios of radio and television live in constant fear of losing their jobs unless, of course, they are outstanding. As a result of these conditions, they are forced to live a political life rather than a musical one. In addition to all of this they are constantly subjected to the temperament and cruelty of the leader. In the symphony orchestra the players have a better musical life because of the beautiful, interesting music they play. But, then there's the conductor. What a monster he can be! Toscannini actually destroyed the confidence of one of the finest clarinetists in the world, simply because he didn't like his phrasing. This could never happen to the Jazz musician. The Jazz musician is his *own* conductor. He is also his own composer. As he grows older, he becomes more of an idol, which, of course, he deserves, having dedicated his life to his music.

JUSTIFIABLE COMPULSION

A well-known jazz musician told me a delightful story about himself. He asked me not to mention his name. He told me that he has a compulsion to gamble and decided to see a psychiatrist. The psychiatrist asked him,

"What is your problem, Mr. X?"

"Well, you see doctor, I've been a gambler all my life and I was hoping that you might cure me of this habit."

"Where do you think the habit came from," asked the doctor.

"My father was a gambler. I suppose I must have got the habit from him," said Mr. X.

"Oh, I don't agree. Your problem goes deeper than that," said the doctor.

"But you don't understand; my father simply told me never to bet on anything that could talk," said Mr. X.

Upon hearing this, the doctor closed his eyes for a couple of minutes giving the appearance of being in a state of deep meditation. When he opened his eyes, he looked at Mr. X and said,

"By God, I believe you have a point."

WE DON'T GO THROUGH THE KITCHEN ANYMORE

Since the beginning of time musicians have been treated no differently than any other kinds of servants. Whenever a band played a party at a posh hotel or home, the maitre d' or the butler would order the musicians around to the back door and through the kitchen. I was not to see the beginning of the end of all this until 1935 when I joined Ray Noble and his orchestra. We were hired to play a party at a townhouse for a leading socialite in New York. Since we played at the Rainbow Room in Rockefeller Plaza until 3 a. m., we were not available to play this party until 4 a. m. When we arrived at the townhouse the butler ordered us around the back through the kitchen. Bill Hardy, the drummer-manager of the band, was furious. He pushed the butler out of the way and said, "You go back to the kitchen and get us some champagne, and make it snappy!" Upon hearing about this, the socialite who hired us asked if we could start playing immediately. "Not until we've had our champagne" replied Bill. The champagne was served and a jolly time was had by all. This must surely have set a precedent. It has become an accepted thing today; drinks are always served before a note is played. I'm speaking only of the posh parties, of course.

The British have a way about them.

JAZZ IS GOOD COLLATERAL

On a recent concert tour of Northern California, we played at the Masonic Auditorium in San Francisco (isn't that a great town?). The hotel in which I stayed didn't carry enough money to cash my check so I took a stroll around the town. I decided to try a bank (banks as a rule have a policy *not* to cash checks for people who have no accounts in them). I presented all the identification I had, but to no avail. As I was leaving the bank, a man just entering it called to me asking if I was Bud Freeman. He was a rabid Jazz fan from London, England. I told him that I had been turned down by the bank and he immediately offered to vouch for me, saying that he had an account there. I, of course, was delighted and thanked him, but he refused to take the position of having done me a favor. He said that he had never hoped to meet me, and that it was *I* who was doing *him* the favor. This, of course, happens to Jazz musicians all over the world and it was not the first time that it happened to me. After getting the money, I offered to buy him a drink; he accepted and took me to an authentic Irish pub that is more than a hundred years old. There is something about the Irish and British pubs that makes drinking such a delight! My British acquaintance and I talked not about music, but rather about all the wonderful people who played it, and then suddenly he said, "You don't talk like a musician — I'd say that you talk more like a writer."

I told him that Nancy Kennedy, the well-known editor had told me the same thing, and that on the strength of what she had said I started to write a book.

"Isn't that interesting? I am also a writer. Is your book about Jazz?" he asked.

"No, I can think of nothing more dull than to write about Jazz. I prefer to write about the people who make the music," I said.

"You've just done me a great service. I was going to

write a book on Jazz theory, but now I think not," he said.

I suggested that Jazz theory would not have got a check cashed for me. He laughed and we had another drink.

SOMETHING IN COMMON

Several years ago, Vic Dickenson (the famous trombone player) and I were playing at a jazz club in Hamilton, Ontario. On our opening night, a white woman came in alone and made quite a play for Vic. A few nights later, a black man came in to see Vic to tell him that the woman was his wife. Vic was taken aback with this news and said,

"Man, she told me you was in jail!"

"She ain't nothing but a white bitch," said the man.

We didn't see the woman again but the man came in every night for the remainder of the engagement. He and Vic became good friends.

THE LOVE LIFE OF A JAZZ MUSICIAN

Rather than embarras the people involved in the following tale, I have decided not to mention any names or places.

Several years ago, I was on tour with the Newport Jazz Allstars. In a small town in the midwest, a press party was given for us. It turned into quite a drunken scene. After having drunk most of the liquor, a beautiful girl introduced herself to me and asked if we could spend the evening together. Since I was between wives at that time (a state I always seem to be in), I naturally accepted this exciting invitation. She suggested a restaurant that she liked and as we were leaving the party, we met her husband who had just arrived with another woman. Since he was in no position to give me a bad time, he bowed and shook my hand very cordially. As my date and I were hailing a taxi, she said, "I wish that I could love my husband. He is such a nice guy." We arrived at the restaurant, took a table and ordered cocktails. Suddenly, her eyes became fixed on a man sitting at a table nearby. His face was buried in his hands, and he appeared to be very drunk. She excused herself, went over to him and upon seeing her, he stood up much quicker than I thought he could.

They embraced and kissed each other madly. She brought him over to meet me and said, "Bud, I'm so sorry. This is my boyfriend." He wasn't as cordial as her husband and I'm not much of a fighter, so I excused myself and left hurriedly. As I was running out of the restaurant, I bumped into a lovely woman who was looking for him. It was *his* wife. I wasn't sure he would have approved of my asking his wife to have a drink and I hope that he didn't go through the difficulty of dodging his wife that I had gone through in dodging him.

A MATTER OF COLOR

I thought about this story for several days before I decided to write it. Any black person who has known me, knows that I am color-blind. I have told this story to many highly educated black friends. They all agreed that I should write it.

I played a concert with the World's Greatest Jazz Band in St. Croix in the Virgin Islands. After the concert, a black gentleman and his lady friend, a black lady, came back stage and invited me to a night club.

The place was packed with swinging, happy people. I was really impressed to see how beautifully the black and white people treated one another. Suddenly, two men sitting next to us (one white, the other black) got into a heated argument. They were very drunk. My two friends became very concerned, thinking, of course, that the argument was racial! I suggested that the two men were just drunk, and that I didn't think the argument had any thing to do with race. My black friend said, rather angrily,

"That's easy for you to say — you're white!"

"But, you're wrong — I'm *not* white," I said.

Of course, I meant that my point of view was not white. Obviously, he thought that I was saying that I was black. He looked at me rather quizzically for a moment and said,

"Do you know that I have a sister who has the same color skin as you."

It turned out that the two drunks shook hands and ordered another drink.

I told this story to Archie Moore, the great prize fighter of yesteryear. He laughed and said,

"You're not white; you're Bud Freeman."

IT WAS NO DIFFERENT THAN WORKING
IN A FACTORY

People have always imagined that musicians, actors and other kinds of show people have a very romantic, fascinating, easy kind of life, but on the contrary, it is at times incredibly laborious. I'll never forget a day with Benny Goodman in 1939. We were working at the Pennsylvania Hotel and doubling at the Paramount Theatre. On one particular day we worked 8 one-hour shows at the theatre, doubled back to the hotel, rehearsed and played the Camel cigarette hour and finished the day with a recording session. In a 24-hour day we actually worked 23 hours. The next day Dave Tough said, "Do you know that every time I sat down yesterday, I was playing the drums."

YOU DON'T HAVE TO BE WHITE TO BE CORNY

For the edification of the Jazz critics who think that one has to be black to play Jazz music, may I suggest that there are many blacks who have no feeling for a Jazz beat at all. One musician in particular was a famous black clarinet player of the twenties; his name was Fess Williams. I shall never forget how shocked I was upon hearing him for the first time. I was very young and naive. I thought that the black musician could do no wrong; so in love was I with his music! Fess, as a clarinet player, was on a par with Ted Lewis the cornball player of all time. Now, one could easily argue that Fess Williams was laughing at the public, but that would have been ridiculous, especially since his audience was strictly black. No, there wasn't the slightest sign of a beat in his body. He would pretend to get his tongue stuck between the reed and the tip of his mouth piece and then pull as though the clarinet would not come out of his mouth. After having been raised on King Oliver and Louis Armstrong, I saw nothing funny in all of this. Of course, it all seems hilarious to me now. Sidney Bechet told me that he played with many black musicians in Europe who actually hated jazz and had no feeling for it. To quote Mary Lou Williams: "Jazz is for everyone to play."

THE GOOD OLD DRINKING DAYS

At the end of the big band era many of the best players

went into the studios — a very lucrative field. Radio, of course, was the popular medium of entertainment featuring shows such as "The Telephone Hour," "The Kate Smith Show," "Report to the Nation," and so on. Two of these best players were Billy Butterfield and Yank Lawson now playing in the World's Greatest Jazz Band. Billy and Yank enjoyed a drink or two and spent a great part of their intermission time at the famous Hurley's Bar and Grill, the favorite drinking place of the musicians, actors, directors, cameramen ,and stagehands at NBC. Billy and Yank commuted every day to their homes on Long Island, but on one particular day, after having had one drink too many, they missed their train. Back to Hurley's for another drink seemed the only logical thing to do — until departure time of their next train. Now Mr. Hurley was not only a fine saloon keeper, he was a good friend. He began to worry about Billy and Yank, and suggested that they have some food and black coffee. Our heroes would have none of it. They drank themselves into a stupor and fell asleep. There they lay in a booth for five hours. When they came out of it, they were told that it was midnight and the last train had left. They called their wives to say that they had a long rehearsal and would be staying at a hotel in town.

With this big problem out of the way, they proceeded to drink again. At 4 a. m., the closing time of the bar, they were stoned again. They were the only people left and Mr. Hurley couldn't talk them into leaving. Suddenly a brilliant idea came into his head. He took their trumpets (in cases, of course) and put them out into the street. When Yank and Billy saw this, they refused to budge unless Mr. Hurley brought back their horns and apologized. As soon as Mr. Hurley went after their horns, they locked him out. Mr. Hurley was not the kind of man to have his friends arrested, so he went home taking their horns with him. He returned at nine o'clock in the morning to find the porter cleaning up the place. Yank and Billy were asleep on the bar. Two empty scotch bottles stood in front of them with a note inside one of them that read: "Dear Mr. Hurley — we couldn't wait for you to return."

B. & Y.

OH, THOSE BANQUETS!

Just recently, we played a benefit performance at a banquet in the Hilton Hotel in New York City. The toastmaster was asked to lead the banqueteers in prayer. He was so drunk that he forgot Christ's first name.

THINGS TO THINK ON

THE TEENAGERS AND JAZZ

For about fifteen years, starting with The Beatles, the teenagers of the world took over the music business. Every living soul had either a banjo or a guitar and, of course, everything was amplified. I speak of this in the past tense because everything in entertainment has its period and then sort of fades out. Most of the Jazz musicians I have known resented all of this, thinking, of course, that it was putting them out of work, but frankly I liked a lot of it. I have always believed that there is room for everything and that if an artist has something creative to say, he's bound to work. The thing that I liked about it all was that for the first time in history millions of young people were beginning to identify with some form of music. Out of all this cacophony some truly talented people have come and I think that much of their music is beautiful.

But now a change has suddenly come. The teenager has begun to listen to Jazz. After all, Jazz is a whole new sound to him. The young cannot be told what to do. They have to feel that they've made a discovery, and if what I've seen in playing concerts around the world in the last year is any indication, millions of young people will become Jazz conscious. This, of course, will give a tremendous amount of work to many great players who've been having a difficult time making a living. Incidentally, people are constantly asking me if I think that the big bands are coming back. Big bands belonged to an era that is gone. Of course, there are several fine big bands that have become institutions and will go on. But, if the people really wanted them to come back they would. It's all a matter of their supporting the idea. In the first place adults have never supported the bands. In the twenties during the big band craze, it was the teenager who supported the bands, just as it is the teenager who buys all the records and supports the music of today. An amusing thing happened one night at a concert in which our band alternated with a very young rock group.

At the end of the concert a kid about sixteen years of age came up to me and said, "Mr. Freeman, my grandfather would like your autograph."

COOL ENOUGH FOR PIANISTS

Yank Lawson tells the delightful story of Jascha Heifetz's debut at Carnegie Hall in New York City. It happened that Mischa Elman, the famous violinist, and Horowitz, the great pianist, were there. After listening to the masterful playing of Heifetz, Mischa Elma took out a handkerchief, wiped his perspired brow, turned to Horowitz and said:

"It's very warm in here."

"Not for pianists," said the great Horowitz.

OVATION TO APATHY

The World's Greatest Jazz Band had just finished a successful tour of Great Britain to standing ovations, and had arrived in Oklahoma City to play at its country club for one night. Our host had paid in advance several thousand dollars for our music, but he hadn't the faintest idea who we were or what we did. As far as he was concerned we could have been a hundred cases of liquor. The first person to greet us was a small nervous, wiry woman reporter who came for an interview. She spotted me first and began her questioning with,

"Are you the world's biggest jazz band?"

"No, madam, we're the world's tiredest jazz band," I said.

"Hmmm," she hummed.

"Can you give me some of the names of the men in the band?"

I gave her every name excepting mine. She hadn't heard of any of us. I thought, wait till she asks me my name — I'll fix her.

"What's your name, sir?" she asked.

"Benny Goodman," I snapped.

"Oh, I thought you were dead," she replied.

"OH, WE FORGOT ABOUT THE MUSICIANS"

There's a legend about a troupe of gypsies that goes

back a few hundred years. It seems that the gypsies had just looted a town of its food, wine and treasures and were about to have a feast when suddenly a group of strangers were seen approaching the gypsy camp. "Hide everything," someone yelled. "Here come the musicians." To this very day I do not think that this myth has been fully dispelled. No matter what the event, whether it be the cost of a road show, the planning of a television show, the organizing of an opera company or a symphonic society, the last expense to be taken into consideration is that of the musicians. One of the most incredible injustices is the planning of a concert auditorium where no thought is given to how the music will sound! How often musicians have to play with pianos that *no one* thought to have tuned. How often producers and advertising agents have thrown money around uselessly with *never* the thought of throwing some of that money to the musician, without whom no entertainment could take place. How often musicians have not been paid for services rendered; it is as if to assume that musicians don't need money — look at all the fun they have playing their instruments. I have known several musicians who stopped playing to go into other businesses — they became millionaires; so easy was it to make money doing something else. If the truth were known, music can be more healthful, at times, than a good meal.

THE CAT THAT HATED JAZZ

I have a cat — a white cat — that weighs thirty pounds. How he became so big I shall never understand. The first time I saw him, he was only five weeks of age and weighed practically nothing, but he had a very lively, happy look about him. I fell in love with him immediately. A boy, about twelve years of age, was playing with the kitten in the street. I told the boy that I wished the kitten were mine. He quickly replied that I could buy the kitten for five dollars. I bought him and took him to my apartment. He took over the place completely. He seemed to ask, "Where is the toilet, where do I sleep, and what time do we eat?" But something was wrong with him; I couldn't get him to eat anything. After a few days of his refusing to eat, I worried that he might die. I took him to the veterinarian, who gave him a shot of something. The shot gave him an appetite and he started to eat the next day. That was ten years ago; he hasn't stopped eating since! In fact, he's a compulsive eater.

He's a loving animal (he never learned to scratch or bite). I tried to take him outside a few times but he seemed to hate it. He's content just to sleep and eat, and to listen to music — not jazz — he hates jazz! Whenever I put on a jazz record, he runs screaming into the night. He loves Beethoven, Brahms, Chopin, Mozart, and Bach. Whenever I play the music of these composers, he plops his polar bear-like body on the floor and swoons. One night as he listened to Mozart, his ears snapped and his eyes nearly popped out of his head. He ran to the record player, jumped on top of it and stopped the record. Now I have not been particularly interested in re-incarnation, but in reading Edgar Casey, I found that Mr. Casey believes that our minds were in other bodies several hundred years ago. If this is true, I wonder if my cat could be Mozart.

THE CUSTOMER IS ALWAYS RIGHT

About fifteen years ago George Wein, the director of the Newport Jazz festival, owned a Jazz club in Boston called Storyville. He booked me there to work as a soloist and on opening night there were quite a few professors sitting up at a table just in front of the bandstand. After the first set they invited me to their table for a drink. We got into a conversation about books and one of the professors said that he was surprised that a jazz musician could be so articulate. Now sitting at a table next to ours was a drunken seaman who was becoming very impatient with our talk, especially since he had come just to hear some jazz music. When he could stand it no longer, he leaned over, tugged on my sleeve and said, "Hey, Bud Freeman, when are you gonna play some goddamn saxophone? You know if you always tell the truth, you don't have to remember what you said."

VULGARITY

As far back as I can remember I have had a guilty feeling about using vulgar language and to this day I feel the same way about it. My father was very much of a Puritan and I do not recall that he ever swore in my presence. I was not to feel differently about it until one night coming home from a concert in New York. My friend who was driving me home was very drunk, going from one side of the street to the other. Surely enough, a very large Rolls Royce towncar sideswiped us and the chauffeur yelled,

"Why don't you get that fuckin' crate off the street," and my friend yelled back,

"Aw go fuck yourself."

Now sitting in the back of this towncar was a very distinguished old lady beautifully coiffeured, with lace collar and lornette, who appeared to be about 80 years of age. Upon hearing all this she put her head out of the window and yelled,

"And fuck you too."

JUST LIKE HOME

The porters at the Century Plaza Hotel in Century City, California are Chinese. Many of them have just come from Hong Kong. They wear uniforms that are exact replicas of what the coolies wore in China. One day I engaged one of the porters in conversation, asking him how he liked being in the United States. He looked at me sadly and said, "Oh sir, all my life I want to come to United States. I get job and they give me the same clothes I had to wear at home."

THE GIBSON GIRLS

In about 1953 I lived in an old fashioned, fashionable hotel in Greenwich Village, called The Van Renselaer. The average aged person living there was about seventy years. It was a delight at dinner time to see these interesting old people, all impeccably dressed as though they were back at the turn of the century. Two ex-Gibson girls, one eighty, the other eighty-four, roomed together and whenever I met them in the lobby or the dining room they had a drink in their hands. They seemed to enjoy talking to me and we became good friends. One day they got pretty drunk in their room and called the manager to send up some ice. The bellboy was out on an errand and the manager, knowing that I was friendly with the old gals, asked me if I would take the ice up to them. As I entered their room, they were arguing with each other and one said to the other, "Agatha, you're drinking that out of the wrong end of the bottle."

I had to go on the road for about a year. Upon returning, I looked into the dining room to say hello to some of my octogenarian friends. There was not a soul there. I asked the manager of the hotel where all of my friends had gone. His immediate reply was, "Oh, Mr. Freeman, everybody died last year."

JEALOUSY — WHAT A STRANGE DISEASE!

I've never been able to understand jealousy. I was shocked to read that the great Tolstoy was jealous of Shakespeare, and went so far as to write that Shakespeare was a bad writer. Emile Zola said that Cezanne had no talent at all. Igor Stravinsky told Pavlova that she couldn't keep time. Toscanini told Galli-Curci that she should have her tonsils put back in, and Wagner said that DeBussy should take some harmony lessons. Now I was amused to read all of this, but I never thought that any of my idols in the jazz world could suffer the same insecurity. During the hegemony of the great Bix, Jack Teagarden came to New York and made quite a splash. One night I asked Bix what he thought of Jack's playing. His answer was angry and direct, "If I want to hear flute, I don't have to listen to it on a trombone." I suppose I was very naive then. How could my idol (the best white Jazz cornet player in the world) be imperfect?

The great Ethel Waters said that Billy Holliday sang as though her shoes were too tight for her. Coleman Hawkins jealously said, "That Lester Young — how does he get away with it? He's stoned half the time — he's always late and he can't play." When Hot Lips Page, the trumpet player, was asked how he liked the way a certain musician played around the melody, he screamed, "That son of a bitch can't find the melody!"

I was raving about Louis Armstrong's playing to Sidney Bechet one night. Sidney surprised me by saying, "Well, I don't know man; I might have some things I want to play too."

I've been playing for forty-eight years; I'm still competing with myself.

HISTORY MAJOR

A few years ago I played a tour of grade schools in the Midwest. Our audiences in attendance were children whose ages ranged from eight to twelve. We played a short Jazz concert, after which we held a sort of jazz clinic where the children asked questions about the instruments we used. One of the teachers, a rabid jazz fan, invited me to his eighth-grade class to witness some of the modern techniques used in teaching history. His subject that day was King Henry the Eighth. After telling his pupils what a monster the king had been, he ended up by saying, "and finally he died of syphilis." A boy sitting in the front row asked, "Is that all he died of, Sir?"

THE SPEEDY HEIFETZ

Yank Lawson, the trumpet player, tells this delightful anecdote about Jascha Heifetz, the great violinist.

Back in the days when the "Telephone Hour" was a radio show on N.B.C., Jascha Heifetz appeared on the show as a soloist. In the middle of his solo, the French horn player in the orchestra, who was very drunk, collapsed. His music stand went flying and his horn slid on the floor striking Heifetz. An emergency squad put the French horn player on a stretcher and carried him out. Heifetz played magnificently through all this. He seemed to be completely impervious to what had happened. Andy Ferretti, the first trumpet player in the orchestra, had discovered a shortcut from N.B.C. to Hurley's Bar and Grill on 49th St. and 6th Avenue. This shortcut was most useful to Andy when, during rehearsals, there was only a five minute break. Now it appeared that he was nursing a two-day hangover — there was a limit to what his nerves could stand. Upon thinking of the French horn player's collapse, Andy rushed down to the bar and ordered a double Scotch. A voice behind him said, "Make that two." Andy turned around to find that the voice belonged to Heifetz. Andy was never able to understand how Heifetz got there so fast.

THE JAZZ CRITIC

Unlike the Broadway theater critic, who has the power to close the show after one performance, the jazz critic is rather ineffectual. If a critic picks on a jazz player, the fans of that player write to the magazine or newspaper, arguing the point and as a result, the controversy gives the player far more publicity than he would have gotten had the critic written a favorable review.

A few years ago, a jazz critic wrote a scathing review about Stan Getz, the great tenor sax player. Stan was deeply offended but I thought that this was a tremendous piece of publicity since it covered about four pages of the *New Yorker* magazine. It was obvious to me that the critic needed something to write about, especially since Stan Getz is considered by the best musical minds in the world to be a great player.

It all reminds me of the time I was leaving Tommy Dorsey's band to join Benny Goodman. The critics were not very happy about my playing and I received more controversial publicity in that short period than in all the years I had been playing. When the controversy ended, I received a call from an agent. This is what he said: "Gee, Bud, you're getting a lot of bad write-ups. Would you like to do a concert tour for our agency?"

ZEN COAN

Zen disciple: "Oh master, what is the opposite of love?"
Zen master: "Arty Shaw on television."

THE MAN WITH THE CLEAR CONSCIENCE

I had just played a concert in Washington, D.C. and boarded the shuttle plane to New York. Sitting in the seat next to me was Adlai Stevenson. He was asleep. About fifteen minutes after takeoff, the flight officers announced that one of the engines had conked out and that we were returning to Washington. Many of the passengers were alarmed and there was a great deal of panic. Mr. Stevenson was awakened by the noise and asked me what was going on. I told him and he said, "Oh, that," whereupon he went back to sleep!

WHAT IS JAZZ?

I have said that I couldn't define Jazz, but that when I heard it for the first time I knew that I was hearing a new form of music. It was like nothing I had heard before. It was lustful, happy, sad and angry — I had the feeling I was playing the music. It appeased all of my needs, making me very happy. To this day, Jazz music has the power to do this to me. Many nights I will go to work feeling despondent but before the night is over the music will give me a tremendous lift.

THEY COULDN'T CARE LESS

Surprisingly enough, there wasn't as much controversy over the name "The World's Greatest Jazz Band" as I thought there would be. Every time that I told people the name of the band, they would invariably ask who was in it. Just recently a jazz critic I had not seen in a long time asked me what I was doing. I told him that I was playing with The World's Greatest Jazz Band." "Oh yeah! Which one?" he asked.

BACKSTAGE AT A JAZZ CONCERT

Jazz reporter: "You all look so happy up on the stage. Are you really that happy?"

Jazz musician: "Well, I don't know. I think it's the money."

ARE THE BIG BANDS COMING BACK?

Several articles have appeared lately in magazines and newspapers, suggesting that, and asking if, the big bands are coming back. Let's examine this. I was there when it all started back in the thirties; I played one-nighters with Tommy Dorsey and Benny Goodman, covering a period of three years. The big band craze started in the eastern seaboard, extending from Maine to Virginia. Most of the places we played were ballrooms, some large enough to hold five thousand dancers. Dancing was the thing, of course; a boy went to meet a girl and a girl went to meet a boy. There were very few adults to be seen. Now the adults of today, who nostalgically talk about the big bands coming back, would be the *last* people to support the bands. They seen to forget that they were teenagers then and that it was quite a thrill to hear these famous bands in person. Today they would prefer to stay at home and watch television. It's true that several big bands are touring the country and drawing crowds, but these are bands that have become institutions. How many are there that work all year round? The demand just isn't there. A few ballroom operators have suggested that big bands are coming back, but where is the money? Bands, today, are forced to take cheap dates just to make traveling expenses. Naturally, the ballroom operator, who had no intention of paying a lot of money in the first place, is going to take advantage of this, the result being that some of the biggest names in the business are working ballrooms for as little as six or seven hundred dollars on a given night. Why shouldn't the operators say that the big bands are coming back? A handful of ballrooms have survived since the thirties because people love to dance; they couldn't care less who is playing. In fact, the simpler the music the better, as far as they are concerned. The big band era lasted about nine years. Once the teenager became an adult, the ballrooms ceased to do the business they needed to pay the big attractions. Thus, the end of an era.

The big band was a thing of its time; it won't be back. One may present the argument: What about Buddy Rich or Woody Herman? Buddy Rich happens to be a tremendous drummer; people would flock to hear him if he had a band of mouth-organs. Woody Herman is a great show-man and a fine guy — people love him. People who wish for the big bands to come back are simply saying, we wish it were 1938 again.

The truth of the matter is that adults have never supported anything. This is strongly evident in the fact that the teenager has taken over the music world. In my travels with The World's Greatest Jazz Band, I've talked to hundreds of people who say that it's good to hear *real* music again, but the *real* music has always been here; the adult did nothing to support it. If the big bands were to make a come-back, they'd have to feature famous soloists with whom the teenager could identify. The teenager today has suddenly become aware of Jazz. Jazz is a brand new sound to him. He is also very aware of the individual soloists in jazz. *No* big band could afford to pay these soloists who make more money than the band leaders. My advice to anyone who wants to start a big band would be to forget it. Of course, if one has a million dollars he can afford to throw away, go ahead.

CAN JAZZ BE TAUGHT?

During the course of writing this book, many people suggested that I explain what Jazz music really is. I think that I've been too close to the music to theorize about it. To begin, I prefer feeling to theory. I have never heard a great player who did not feel what he was doing. How can one be taught to feel music? I suggested earlier that the best players all listened to the recordings of the masters, borrowing what ideas they liked to develop their own styles. All great players are natural; I do not see how they can impart (in words, that is) what they are doing. The greatest joy in learning how to play is in listening to records. I can never forget what a thrill it was to hear a new recording of Louis Armstrong or Bix, or Fats Waller, or Art Tatum. We used to have sessions of listening and discussing musical ideas that lasted for hours on end. I think that this is the only way to learn anything about Jazz music. If one feels the music, what could be more natural? If one doesn't feel the music, of what value are words?

ZEN AND THE JAZZ MUSICIAN

It has been said: "Although man is a thinking reed, he does his best work when he isn't thinking." This is absolutely true of the jazz player. In the twenties the great Louis Armstrong was recording a tune called "The Heebie Jeebies." As he was singing the words of the song he dropped the piece of music and continued as though nothing had happened by singing improvised notes that developed into a completely original Jazz form of improvised singing.

SPORTS

Dick Gibson, our ex-manager, tells a delightful story about a gigantic football player and a little coach. The coach, in trying to instill some sort of winning spirit into his team, yelled at the giant:

106

"If I were you, I could be the heavyweight champion of the world!!" The giant's rebuttal was, "Yeah? Well why ain't ya the lightweight champion of the world?"

FUTURE PRAYER

Now I lay me down to sleep.
I pray to Freud my soul to keep.
If I should dream before I wake,
I certainly hope so for my psychiatrist's sake.

MAKE MINE GENUINE

For the last thirty years, jazz critics and jazz musicians have been criticizing players whose styles never changed. In my opinion it takes a lifetime to develop a style of playing that one may call his own. If an artist is genuine, his work lives through all the stages of criticism.

Just recently I spent an evening with a friend who has a large collection of jazz records. I was amazed to hear how fresh Louis Armstrong's records of the early twenties sound today; how Bix's playing holds up; and Fats Waller seems to be with you in person. People are constantly asking me what's going to happen to jazz music when all the greats are gone? They've been asking that question for years on end, and look at all the great players who have come up in the last thirty years. What's more, we'll always have the recordings. Jazz is here to stay. As regards genuine, creative playing, the player is on his own. If he changes his style every six months, as many players do, he's never going to create anything! It may take a long time, but in finality, it's worth it. There is no *one* way to play; we all hear and feel differently. Listen to everything and make up your *own* mind. Learning how to play is the most interesting experience of all.

JAZZ NEVER LEFT

Everywhere I play people ask me if I think jazz is coming back. I don't think that *it* ever left. Jazz has never really been exploited; that is, the publicity has always been given to the band or group leader. Now, finally the soloists are becoming famous. People all over the world are asking about the individual soloists, and very little about the leaders. In the days of the big bands, the creative players in these bands were just side men and very little attention was paid to the wonderful things they played. The leaders took all the credit, and when these bands broke up, the public thought that jazz was dying — but no one stopped to think that the soloists went right on creating new jazz ideas. They played in the worst kinds of dives just to be doing what they loved to do best. In many cases they played for nothing and, of course, the owners of these dives took advantage of this by putting a sign in the window which simply read: "Jam session tonight." But the music *never* stopped; nor will it *ever* stop. Jazz doesn't need theme or melody. It is its own theme and melody. It doesn't need direction. It is its own direction. This is how it differs from other kinds of music.

Is jazz coming back? It *never* left.

HERE AND THERE

NO, NO NANETTE

I went to see the road company of "No, No Nanette." The show was playing in Detroit where I've been working on this book. I had no particular motivation to see it (I'm not interested in nostalgia) but my old friend, Gil Bowers, was working in the show as pianist-conductor. Gil is a fine musician who played with the top bands of the thirties. I was pleasantly surprised to find that it is an *excellent* show. First of all, Vincent Youman's music holds up; "I Want to Be Happy" and "Tea for Two" have been standards for more than thirty years. The costumes are the *finest* I've ever seen and the dancers are far superior to the dancers in the original cast of 1925.

An extraordinary thing happened near the end of the show. The audience, twenty-one-hundred strong, struck up a unison hand-clapping that seemed to say, "this is our music." This has never happened in a musical comedy audience that was predominately white. Of course, the black people have been doing this in their churches since the beginning of time. Why do white people invariably clap on the beat? Oh well, I suppose I should be grateful that the beat is finally getting to them in some way.

THE M. C.

In the last few months of 1942 (just before going into the Army), I had a band at the Sherman Hotel in Chicago. We played in the Panther Room that featured dancing, a floor show and an M. C.

The M. C. was the son of a wealthy man, a friend of the maitre d'. Obviously, the boy had to use his father's influence to get the job, since he hadn't the slightest bit of talent. He just wanted to be in show business, which he thought to be very glamorous. His simple job each night was to introduce the band, the principals in the show, and to make announcements of the forthcoming bands. Now, since he believed that show business was a "fun" sort of thing and not a hard, cold business, he drank all the liquor he could find. It appeared that Jan Savitt, a famous bandleader of the forties, was to be the next attraction in the Panther Room. This is how our drunken M. C. announced the forthcoming appearance of the band:

"Ladies and Gentlemen: Starting on Jan the Savitt, we will have June 7th and her orchestra."

Luckily for our M. C., he went into business with his father. I saw him just recently. He hasn't changed. "Oh, how I miss show business!" he sighed.

THE IGNORANT CAN BE FUNNY

I was taking a cab from the airport to a hotel in Dallas, Texas. I asked the driver how the people were getting along (meaning, of course, the blacks and whites).

"We don't stand for no trouble out this way. Just the other day two of them edicated niggers came into town and tried to stir up some trouble, but they didn't git anywhere," he drawled.

"Who were they?" I asked.

"They were James Farmer and Hoagy Carmichael," he replied.

THE MOVIE CRITIC

When the film "Mr. Chips" first opened in New York, it opened in a little theatre just next door to a burlesque show. I bought a seat in the balcony and about five minutes before the film came on, a staggering drunk fell on me and sat there as though he thought I was his seat. He was a little man so I had no difficulty in placing him in his own seat. The film started and (what with the soft theme music and introductory names of its actors) my friend's drunkenness seemed to turn into a state of impatience, whereupon he turned to me and said, "Hey buddy, ain't this no burlesque show?"

THE ACTORS

Just recently I went to see a movie in Beverly Hills. About ten minutes before the film came on, the lights were turned up. In the row in front of me, three children were jumping around in their seats. They looked enough alike to be brothers. I asumed that the eldest was about twelve years of age and the others about ten. I was shocked to see that they were wearing make-up and that their eyebrows were tweezed. They appeared never to be looking at anyone, but rather, they looked off into space as though they expected a television talent scout to discover them at any moment. I couldn't wait for the movie to end.

MUHAMMED ALI: PUBLIC RELATIONS GENIUS

The first time I met Ali was at the Ohio Valley Jazz Festival. I was playing with the Newport Allstars, which drew a crowd of about 15,000 people. Some of the stars were Miles Davis, Dave Brubeck, Ruby Braff, Pee Wee Russell and Jerry Mulligan.

Suddenly, out of nowhere, came Ali. He walked up on the bandstand, unannounced, pounding his chest and roaring, "I am the greatest, I am the greatest." Since I had never seen him before, I wasn't certain whether or not he was clowning. I was not to find out until the next day in the lobby of the hotel. We had all stayed for the night. He was sitting on a table, autographing cards, books, and what-not for hundreds of admirers who recognized him. As I passed by to say "hello" to him, he smiled and said, "Beautiful music, beautiful music." What a pleasant person, I thought. I'd like to talk to him. After the autograph seekers left, I walked up to him and said,

"What's all this newspaper talk about you being a bragging bore? You're not like that at all." He laughed and said,

"You know, man, that's my gimmick."

I talked to him for about 15 minutes and found him to be one of the brightest, kindest and most sincere men I have ever met.

That was several years ago. I did not meet him again until recently. We were appearing on the Mike Douglas show. Mike was on vacation and Howard Cosell was guest host. Before Howard and Ali made their appearance, they had a rehearsal in the wings. This is what I heard Ali say:

"Howard, we're the biggest attraction in show business.

Let's get a little more hatred in our conversation. The people will eat it up."

They came on the air, Ali insulted Howard with every word he could think to say. The people ate it up!

CATEGORIES

Jazz must be the most powerful of all music. For at least seventy years it has endured in spite of all the ridiculous titles given it. It has been called New Orleans, Chicago, West Coast, Bebop, Main Stream Avant-Garde, Modern, Dixieland, and you name it. These titles, of course, were never invented by musicians who must surely have thought they were pretty funny. The unfortunate thing about all of this was that fine players were put into categories and actually could not get any work if the agents didn't like the category the musician was put into. One such agent who, of course, knew nothing about Jazz music, called me about opening at a jazz club and asked what I played. Did I play modern or dixieland? My simple reply was, "I play beautifully."

THE CAP

On a recent concert tour with The World's Greatest Jazz Band, our bus driver (one of the most unique bus drivers I've ever met), actually went out of his way to make us comfortable in every way. Some of the distances from town to town were quite long, but he refused to take the easy way out by stopping to rest or sleep. As a result of this, we always arrived at our destination with plenty of time to get a full night's rest. He was also an excellent driver and never took any risks to make time. He was immaculately dressed, always clean-shaven, and he wore a very smart cap that gave him the appearance of a German military officer out of the First World War. One of the most successful concerts on the tour was played at Virginia Military Institute in Lexington, Virginia. Having played at many military schools, I can testify that the manners of the cadets at V.M.I. were the most impeccable. Our bus driver always took it upon himself to help in carrying our luggage and instruments into the motels and places we played. On this particular night he entered the hall first and the cadets upon seeing this miiltary-like cap,

113

came to attention, throwing him a very smart salute, whereupon he commanded, "At ease!" He told me later that it was worth the whole trip.

THE MOVIES

I saw the film, "The Godfather," today. It is a masterpiece! Not because of its authenticity regarding the Italian underworld, but because of its director. Mr. Coppolla is a great artist! It is not enough to say that Marlon Brando is a great actor — I was convinced that I was seeing a real Don in action. Brando did not resort to the obvious Italian accent, which he could have done, but rather to a kind of voice that one could readily understand would be the voice of a man who had lived through many years of such a life. I believe that the film has a message to offer. It is better to know that such an underworld exists, than to live in doubtful fear of it. I came out of the theatre with a feeling of enlightenment.

HOW TO PLAY THE HORSES

Many words have been written and much has been said about extra-sensory-perception, and I'm certain that there's a great deal of validity in it. But I've found a much more useful thing called "extra-sensory horseception." Many years of playing the horses has lessened my confidence in man — I mean the little man called the jockey. I don't think that I've ever known a dishonest horse. One day many years ago at the old Belmont Track in New York, I was standing in line to make a bet at the ten-dollar window. Just in front of me stood a little lady who appeared to be about seventy years old. She bought two ten dollar tickets on a 70-1 shot and as she turned to leave I asked,

"Madam, how can you bet twenty dollars on a 70-1 shot?" Her reply was simple and sweet:

"Oh, young man, I'm not interested in the odds. I just like the horse's name."

I, of course, with my racing form in hand, bet on the favorite. The race was off and the 70-1 shot won by two lengths and paid $143.60. I was so angry with myself for not playing the long shot that I tore up everything I had on me that looked like paper. I have never looked at a racing form since. The next day on the track train, a drunk brushed by me yelling, "Hey Mac in the first; can't lose." As soon I got to the track I rushed out to the paddock to see an old tout I'd known for years. I asked about the horse "Hey Mac" and the tout's quick reply was, "the horse's lame. He'll probably be scratched." I decided to look at the horse anyway. I looked him over very carefully and he was, indeed, lame. Do I stay with the "extrasensory horseception" or do I take the advice of the tout? Suddenly a flash came to me — the horse wasn't lame he was doped. That was all I had to know. I ran out and looked at the odds. "Hey Mac" was 50-1. I put ten dollars on his nose. They were off and he broke out in front and led all the way to a 5½-length win. I went completely out of my mind, jumping up and down with my win ticket, telling everybody about it. When I finally calmed down I began to reason that if I let anyone else in on this, all of my 50-1 shots would be going off at 1-10. Not until now have I divulged this information. I could list a hundred names of longshots that have won for me over the years — they still do. One day my tout friend asked,

"What do ya do on a day when all the favorites win?" My ready answer was,

"I don't play that day."

Incidentally, I don't think that favorites have "extrasensory-horseception." That's why they don't win.

A PLACE TO PLAY

Just after the St. Valentine's Day massacre, Al Capone became the undisputed boss of the Chicago underworld. He owned a string of bars, nightclubs, gambling casinos, and what not on the south side. One such nightclub was a place I played in called Charlie's. It was in an old stone building in a section that looked like a bombed out area. Inside the building was a very posh restaurant and nightclub. The bar was half a block long. It was beautifully polished so that the bartender could slide drinks down it, and there were excellent paintings of nude women hanging on the wall. The nightclub had a small bandstand and dance floor. Dave Tough and I worked there in a five-piece Jazz band. Now in those days many of the places that Jazz musicians could play were owned by

Capone. The better hotels and restaurants employed violinists and pianists who played what we thought to be very old-fashioned music. We were happy to have a place to play the kind of music we loved.

The part-owner of the club was an ex-heavyweight prizefighter by the name of Dick Hans. He was a Capone lieutenant. At one time he had been the sparring partner of Jess Willard, the man who took the title away from the great Jack Johnson, from whose life "The Great White Hope" was taken. Dick was a giant who stood six-feet-five-inches tall and weighed two hundred and twenty pounds. He had two enormous cauliflower ears, two swollen lips, and a smashed nose. Whenever he engaged anyone in conversation, he'd give an exhibition of some of his previous fights. He was quite punch-drunk. He told us that every time he sparred with Jess Willard he'd knock him down and Jess would get up and say, "Hey, I'm the champ, not *you*." Dave Tough weighed 100 lbs. Dick used to call him "Damn Tough."

Most of the customers were gunmen who came in late, checked their ammunition behind the bar and went into the nightclub to dine and dance with the hostesses. They were very polite; I never saw a fight in the place. Now since prohibition was still the law, the club employed a lookout man by the name of "Little Anthony." Little Anthony was a very small, wiry man. He stood at the end of the bar and never took his eyes off of the door. He could smell a federal agent a block away and he knew every gunman in town. One night two holdup men came into the bar carrying shotguns. They ordered all of us to put our hands up. We all obeyed except Little Anthony. He very casually walked over to the holdup men and said, "Don't you guys know whose joint this is?" They looked at each other and turned to leave. Little Anthony called after them to wait. He then walked over to the bar and asked the bartender for two twenty-dollar bills. He gave each man one of the bills and they left. Later that night I asked him why he gave them the money and he said, "It was for their effort." These men had simply walked into the wrong place. Three nights later they came back as customers and bought the house a round of drinks.

Joe Marsala ,the well-known Chicago clarinetist, will vouch for what I've written here. He and I played together in many of these places.

In the fifty years that Dick Hans lived in Chicago, he never ventured north of the Chicago River. His favorite expression was, "They'll never catch me over there with my guns down."

If Jazz music could only talk, what stories it could tell!

DILLINGER

Sitting in the bleachers at the ball game one day, I met a delightful old man who at one time had been Dillinger's lawyer. Of course, I was curious to know what this man thought of the notorious bank robber of the thirties. In answer to my query, he said: "Oh, John wasn't a bad fellow. You have to remember that he never shot his way *into* a bank!"

MUSICIANS SOOTHE THE COPS

Musicians of the twenties and thirties seemed never to be addicted to anything but the music they played and were constantly going places to hear other musicians play and to hold jam sessions, no matter where. One such jam session took place in a house called in those days a "good time flat." This was during prohibition and, of course, when the $ police were not paid off, there were constant raids on these flats. They usually sold home-made wine and liquor. At about 3:00 a. m. at this particular session, the police, instead of knocking on the door, simply knocked it down and took all of us in what was then called the paddy wagon. On our way down to the police station, we continued our jam session in the paddy wagon since we knew we hadn't done anything wrong. Since this must surely have been a first of its kind, the police were completely dumbfounded and didn't know what to do about it. The desk sergeant said: "Get those musicians out of here before they wreck this jail house!"

EVER THE TWAIN SHALL BEAT

When Mark Twain was lecturing at colleges and universities, he always advised students *not* to let college get in the way of education. Mark would be delighted to see the great change that has taken place. I have played about thirty colleges in the last year and the deans, presidents, and professors are all long-haired, mod-dressed, swinging lovers of jazz music. Since jazz is now being taken seriously in many schools, I have been invited to many classes to witness some of the new techniques in teaching. Some teachers actually play jazz records in their classes. One day in a poetry reading class, the professor was upset with a student whose reading was very poor. "Can't you sing it out with a beat?", he pleaded. "Listen to the way Louie Armstrong does it!"

THE SCENE IS JAZZ — JULY 3, 1972

Earlier in this book, I mentioned that the teenager was beginning to identify with jazz. I did not realize at that time, since that was several months ago, that his devotion to amplified music would end so soon. Now after twelve years, it would appear that he has turned to jazz. When one realizes that there are hundreds of thousands of teenagers around the world who are bound to follow one another, the sales of jazz records could become astronomical. I saw evidence of this last night at the Music Hall Theater in New York City. The Music Hall features the current movies and a commercial stage presentation. It has catered to a public that believes that anything the Music Hall presents must be good entertainment. What a thrill it was to see a line of young people waiting to get into the theater to hear jazz music. The Newport Jazz Festival had come to town. Vic Dickenson and I were invited to play this great festival, which started at midnight. Our band was made up of several world-famous soloists: Gene Krupa, Teddy Wilson, Red Norvo, Larry Ridley, Jim Hall, Benny Carter, Bobby Hacket and Roy Eldridge. We played four jazz standards and received a standing ovation just doing our thing. It took a long time coming, but jazz is here to stay!

I CAN'T THINK OF A BETTER LIFE

Mothers, whose sons have a desire to play musical instruments, are constantly asking me if I think it a good idea. (Isn't the life difficult? Aren't the hours bad for one's health? Isn't it difficult to make a living?) The questions are endless and naive, but rather than be rude, I always answer by saying that one plays an instrument because one must. Every creative player I've ever known had to play music as one has to eat. The desire to play music burns deeply inside of a man. If the potential player doesn't have this feeling, what difference does it make? He'll soon find out that music is not for him; the worst thing that can happen is that he'll have the joyful experience of trying to play. As regards the kind of life, I can speak only for myself. I love golf, I love to walk, I love all outside sports; I spend more time outside than the average person, no matter what kind of work he does. It is true that it's difficult to make a living at times, but this rarely enters the mind of one who wants to play badly enough. I have never known a great player who didn't receive the opportunity to make a good living. I have lived all over the world; I've met every walk of life from the poorest to the richest; I've met the most famous people in the world including Royalty and the notorious. I can't think of a better life.